# E-made Easy
## INTERNET MLM TACTICS

**BY**
**Charles "Tremendous" Jones**
**& Gerald Robinson**

ExecutiveBooks.com • Mechanicsburg, PA

## You are the same today as You will be in five years except for three things:
## The People You Meet
## The Books You Read
## and Your
# TECH-KNOWLEDGE

First Edition 1999
ExecutiveBooks.com
A division of Executive Books
206 West Allen Street
Mechanicsburg, PA 17055
800-233-2665
www.executivebooks.com / www.tremendousjones.com

Printed in the United States of America

ISBN: 0-937539-40-6
LLCN # 99-68635

**EB**

**Executive Books**

# Introduction

The high tech/high touch revolution is here and network marketers across the world are looking for ways to capitalize on the amazing success technology can bring them. Until today, few books have helped them use the computer and the Internet to attain financial freedom.

Network marketers need tools to help them successfully maintain a hands-on approach with their customers, prospects, and distributors. This means that technology must help them communicate better, support their personal interaction with people and save them time.......lots of time.

People don't have the time to understand a computer guide that reads like a textbook. They simply need a resource that gives them a concept, provides them the application, and then tells them how to do it. E-Made Easy contains these methods, and more, including ways to reduce marketing costs and greatly increase communication efficiency by featuring unique and specific methods never before documented in a book of this kind.

The key ingredient, which has been missing, is training. In a time when most executives are hoping that the creative person shows the rest of the force the way, the time has come for a structured program on how to use the computer as network marketers should use it.

This book will explain the ways the computer can be used to increase prospect pools, increase revenue and decrease costs. The computer has been taught, re-taught, explained and highlighted as a tool a person can use, however, never like this has there ever been a more specific assembly of ways to use the computer in the process by the network marketer .

For the best results read the book while at a computer. Enjoy the book and remember cyber-sales is the information age way!

# TABLE OF CONTENTS

**Chapter**            **Page Number**

INTRODUCTION . . . . . . . . . . . . . . . . . . . . . . . . . . . . . . . .1
TABLE OF CONTENTS . . . . . . . . . . . . . . . . . . . . . . . . . . .2
PROLOGUE . . . . . . . . . . . . . . . . . . . . . . . . . . . . . . . . . . .5
1. E-Mail: The Arm that Reaches . . . . . . . . . . . . . . . . . . .13
  How to Structure an E-mail Letter . . . . . . . . . . . . . . . . .15
  Including Company Information Via Hyperlinks . . . . . . . . . . . .16
    • *Helpful Hint:* How to Make a Hyperlink . . . . . . . . . . . . . . . .16
  How to Hyperlink Specific Pages within a Website . . . . . . . . . .17
  Hyperlinking from Your Company's Website vs.
  Sending Brochures or Materials . . . . . . . . . . . . . . . . . .18
  Hyperlinking References from The Web . . . . . . . . . . . . . . .18
    • *Helpful Hint:* Finding Reference Links . . . . . . . . . . . . . .19
  Sending E-mail Before Meetings . . . . . . . . . . . . . . . . . .20
  Signatures . . . . . . . . . . . . . . . . . . . . . . . . . . . . .22
    • *Helpful Hint:* Creating Signatures . . . . . . . . . . . . . . . . .23
  Using Signatures to Quickly Make E-mails . . . . . . . . . . . . .24
  E-mail PowerPoint Presentations as Attachments . . . . . . . . . . .25
    • *Helpful Hint:* Animating Objects in PowerPoint
    for a Presentation . . . . . . . . . . . . . . . . . . . . . . . . .26
    • *Helpful Hint:* Saving PowerPoint as a Show . . . . . . . . . . . .27
  How to Find Your Prospect's E-mail Address . . . . . . . . . . . .28
    • *Helpful Hint:* Message Rejection Notices . . . . . . . . . . . . .30
  Address Book . . . . . . . . . . . . . . . . . . . . . . . . . . . .30
    • *Helpful Hint:* Mailing Lists . . . . . . . . . . . . . . . . . . .30
  Adding to the Address Book . . . . . . . . . . . . . . . . . . . . .31
  E-mail Filters . . . . . . . . . . . . . . . . . . . . . . . . . . .32
    • *Helpful Hint:* Creating New Folders in Your Inbox . . . . . . . .33
    • *Helpful Hint:* Creating Mail Filters . . . . . . . . . . . . . . .33
  Responding to Your Customer's E-mail
  While You're Away at a Meeting or on Vacation . . . . . . . . . . .34
    • *Helpful Hint:* Setting Up Out-of-the-Office Replies . . . . . . . .35

2. Browser Power! . . . . . . . . . . . . . . . . . . . . . . . . . . . .37
  Where the Browser Can Help . . . . . . . . . . . . . . . . . . . .38
  Copy and Paste . . . . . . . . . . . . . . . . . . . . . . . . . . .38

Copying Links . . . . . . . . . . . . . . . . . . . . . . . . . . . . . . . .39
  • *Helpful Hint:* How to Copy a Website Address
  from the Title Bar . . . . . . . . . . . . . . . . . . . . . . . . . . .39
Use Material from Websites in Presentations
and to Address Quotes & Letters . . . . . . . . . . . . . . . . . . . . . .40
Copying E-mail Addresses . . . . . . . . . . . . . . . . . . . . . . . . . .40
A Picture is Worth a Thousand Words . . . . . . . . . . . . . . . . . . .41
  • *Helpful Hint:* Saving and Inserting Pictures . . . . . . . . . . . . .41
  • *Helpful Hint:* Where to Find Good Pictures . . . . . . . . . . . . .42
  • *Helpful Hint:* Website Text Copy/Paste Example . . . . . . . . .42
Sitemarking . . . . . . . . . . . . . . . . . . . . . . . . . . . . . . . . . .42
  • *Helpful Hint:* Menu Picks to Create Sitemark Files . . . . . . .43
Naming Sitemark Files . . . . . . . . . . . . . . . . . . . . . . . . . . . .44
Deciding on What to Sitemark . . . . . . . . . . . . . . . . . . . . . . .44
  • *Helpful Hint:* Organizing Sitemarks . . . . . . . . . . . . . . . . .45
Copying Sitemark Files into E-mail to Save Time . . . . . . . . . . . .46
  • *Helpful Hint:* Sitemarks Managers . . . . . . . . . . . . . . . . . .47
Making Hyperlink Summary Sheets . . . . . . . . . . . . . . . . . . . .47
  • *Helpful Hint:* Creating Hyperlinks Summary Sheets . . . . . . .48
Sitemarks Saved and Sent . . . . . . . . . . . . . . . . . . . . . . . . .52
  • *Helpful Hint:* Sending Sitemarks . . . . . . . . . . . . . . . . . . .52
History Files . . . . . . . . . . . . . . . . . . . . . . . . . . . . . . . . .54
Finding Valuable Sites that You Have Visited
but Didn't Sitemark . . . . . . . . . . . . . . . . . . . . . . . . . . . . .54
  • *Helpful Hint:* History Search . . . . . . . . . . . . . . . . . . . . . .55

3. Mission: Re"Search" and Enjoy . . . . . . . . . . . . . . . . . . . . . .57
Search Engines . . . . . . . . . . . . . . . . . . . . . . . . . . . . . . . .58
  • *Helpful Hint:* Narrow Your Search . . . . . . . . . . . . . . . . . .59
Information on The Web . . . . . . . . . . . . . . . . . . . . . . . . . . .60
Companies at A Glance . . . . . . . . . . . . . . . . . . . . . . . . . . .63

4. Prospecting: The New Fashioned Way . . . . . . . . . . . . . . . . . .65
Internet Phone Books . . . . . . . . . . . . . . . . . . . . . . . . . . . .66
Finding People . . . . . . . . . . . . . . . . . . . . . . . . . . . . . . . .70
  • *Helpful Hint:* Source Sites . . . . . . . . . . . . . . . . . . . . . . .70
Pre-Planning Your Week . . . . . . . . . . . . . . . . . . . . . . . . . .72

5. Unique uses of Word and Excel as Network Marketing Tools . . . .75

Excel in Network Marketing . . . . . . . . . . . . . . . . . . . . . . . . . . . .76
Use Spreadsheets to Be More Efficient . . . . . . . . . . . . . . . . . . . .76
   • *Helpful Hint:* Inserting Addition, Subtraction,
Multiplication and Division Functions . . . . . . . . . . . . . . . . . . .81
ROI's (Return on Investment) and Justifications . . . . . . . . . . . .81
More Excel Time Saving Tricks . . . . . . . . . . . . . . . . . . . . . . . . .83
Competitive Placement Summary Spreadsheets . . . . . . . . . . . . . .83
   • *Helpful Hint:* Hyperlinks in Excel and PowerPoint . . . . . . . . .85
   • *Helpful Hint:* Creating AutoFilters . . . . . . . . . . . . . . . . . . . . .86
Other Excel-Lent Features . . . . . . . . . . . . . . . . . . . . . . . . . . . . .86
Comments in Word and Excel . . . . . . . . . . . . . . . . . . . . . . . . . .87
   • *Helpful Hint:* Creating Comments . . . . . . . . . . . . . . . . . . . . . .88

6. Information Age Marketing . . . . . . . . . . . . . . . . . . . . . . . . . . . .91
Internal Website . . . . . . . . . . . . . . . . . . . . . . . . . . . . . . . . . . . .92
Sales and Marketing . . . . . . . . . . . . . . . . . . . . . . . . . . . . . . . . .92
Presentation Tools . . . . . . . . . . . . . . . . . . . . . . . . . . . . . . . . . . .94
Prospecting Tools . . . . . . . . . . . . . . . . . . . . . . . . . . . . . . . . . . .95
   • *Helpful Hint:* Technology Business Browser Suggestion . . . . .95
Competition . . . . . . . . . . . . . . . . . . . . . . . . . . . . . . . . . . . . . . . .96
Training . . . . . . . . . . . . . . . . . . . . . . . . . . . . . . . . . . . . . . . . . . .96
Training Material . . . . . . . . . . . . . . . . . . . . . . . . . . . . . . . . . . . .97
Training Course Schedules . . . . . . . . . . . . . . . . . . . . . . . . . . . . .97
Intranet Sales Administrations . . . . . . . . . . . . . . . . . . . . . . . . . .97
External Website . . . . . . . . . . . . . . . . . . . . . . . . . . . . . . . . . . . .97

7. Hints and Lists . . . . . . . . . . . . . . . . . . . . . . . . . . . . . . . . . . . . .101
Information Age Hints . . . . . . . . . . . . . . . . . . . . . . . . . . . . . . .102
Websites Every Network Marketer Should Know About . . . . . . .103

# Prologue

I was driving down the road with my brother one day in late 1997. We were having one of those heated debates that convinced my parents that my brother and me were somehow not related. The debate was about sales people who use old fashioned tactics. Are they effective? Do salespeople need to change from the old ways?

My brother has done great for himself. In his eight year career he has gone from an entry level position to a Vice President. In his present position he deals with salespeople every day.

He gets calls from anyone from paper salesmen to financial software "consultants."

**Joe Salesman:** Mr. Robinson, hello, my name is Joe Salesman. I am the division manager for Financial Disk America. In your line of business, financial, you must deal with taxes. Is that correct Mr. Robinson?

**Mr. Robinson:** Joe, that is a very good observation (Who is this rocket scientist?).

**Joe Salesman:** Our customer, NBC company, was able to save $400,000 last year when they capitalized on using our software. Right now I have a person in the area who can stop by and see you this afternoon. Will two o'clock or three o'clock be O.K. for you?

**Mr. Robinson:** Well, I am really busy this afternoon. However, this is your lucky day. My brother is a salesman and I really have a heart for you guys. Why don't you come in tomorrow at 10:30 a.m.

Well, it turned out that the person did stop-by. My brother told the person that the software could be useful in his company but the timing was wrong. He would keep them in mind.

As salespeople we all know the companies for which we distribute will not take "the timing is wrong" as an excuse. We all know we will hear:

"You could have done better."
"Why didn't you try this?"
"When are you calling them back?"
"The competition is probably in there right now."

A month later the division manager called my brother again. He proceeded to tell him that he had a person in the area and could have her stop by that afternoon. My brother told him that he just went through this last month and told the person that his company was in the process of being sold and he couldn't undertake a major project at the time. He asked the manager, "Didn't your sales person tell you about our meeting last month?" The manager responded with the smooth response "uh uh uh uh uh uh..."

The manager slid off the mistake like a pro. He immediately went into a line of questioning to find out what was ticking in my brother's mind. He wanted to start off innocently enough. He said "Mr. Robinson, how many offices do you have and what exactly do they do?"

**Mr. Robinson:** "Look Joe, I told you I wasn't interested. Thanks for your call..." CLICK!

This is a close-to-the-heart story for me. I, of course, defended my profession. I would never let my brother get away with busting my sales brethren. So, I began my defense.

"You don't know what it is like in the world of sales. Some people always expect perfection. That manager probably has 20 sales people underneath him and can't keep track of every person he calls. When you have a monster quota sitting in front of you given by an executive who thinks making quota is 80 cold calls a day, you occasionally have to push."

My brother didn't argue with that. His beef was with the manager's question: *"By the way, how many offices does your company have and what do they do?"*

You see, my brother had a point that we, as sales people, should realize. His main impression was that the sales person who was calling him was unprepared. His reasoning was that, not only did they not know how many offices his company had, but they didn't even know what they did.

You see, that information, as my brother so eloquently put it, "IS ALL ON THE INTERNET AND THE SALES PERSON WAS EXPECTED TO KNOW IT BEFORE THE CALL!"

## Old Fashioned Sales Methods

While I was deciding in which direction to take this book, I reviewed some of the old closes that had been taught to me when I was just a greenhorn sales person. Following are some examples of closes used in the past:

### *"The Porcupine Close"*

The porcupine is the technique of answering a question with a question of your own that maintains your control of the interview and allows you to lead into the next step of your selling sequence.

An example of the close is:

*Sales person: "Won't people be annoyed unless I give them specific answers to their questions?"*

*Porcupine answer from sales manager: "Why are you so fearful of annoying people when your main concern should be to close business so that they can start to enjoy the benefits of your offering?"*

Let me make this clear. Don't ever use the **porcupine close.** Don't ever refer to the **porcupine close.** The sales person that uses this close in their arsenal had better be selling something no one else has, giving money to the purchasing agent, or dating the president's daughter.

Let's try another:

### *"The Standard Tie Down"*

*The tie-down is a question that closes out a sentence to help gain agreement which is meant to help in advancing the sale, such as:*

*Sales Person: "Low electricity cost is very important today, isn't it?"*

*If the prospect sees this as true, the person supposedly responds by agreeing. Agreement on some quality of your product or service that meets their needs, means they've moved closer to buying it.*

The real tragedy of these methods is that there is some merit to what is presented. Sales is a function of questioning, it is a function of assuming and leading, and it is a function of closing. However, it is not a game played by stupid people. The 1990's environment doesn't have a lot of stupid people in purchasing positions, waiting for the sly, practiced, and smart network marketer to throw the Standard Tie-down on them so they'll buy like ignorant zombies with huge checkbooks, does it?

Today's network marketer has major competition that know the same basic sales tactics that they do. The Standard Tie-down doesn't differentiate anymore. Allow me to rephrase the previous sentence. The Standard Tie-down does differentiate you—negatively. These basic, bush league sale tactics have been around for ages. They started back when Eli Whitney was slinging the Cotton Gin door to door. It started when the average person barely knew how to read. It started when unleaded gas was in the form of hay at the local stable. After using the Standard Tie-down when would you like most to lose your customer's respect, today or next week?

You may ask: "Why should I change my selling style when so many professionals today still use these methods?"

I say to you: "Why are you so focused on the status quo when you should be more concerned with making more money?"

Somehow these methods have stuck around for the ages. Continually cultivated by evermore aggressive salespeople who learned from their teachers, who learned from their teachers, that this was the right way to sell:

TRAINER: *"The prospect doesn't know what he wants yet, but with your skills you'll get him."*

SALES PERSON: *"I closed him today, it was classic. I said, 'Would you like delivery today, or tomorrow.' I fooled the prospect into the right decision."*

These are common phrases in an uncommon time, the Information Age.

The old ways have conditioned an ever smarter buying pool to believe that we are a bunch of actors, thieves with a license to steal, double OO sales person, "The name is Robinson. Gerry Robinson."

- The average American watches 28 hours of television per week.
- As of mid-1998 more than 70,000,000 Americans have access to the Internet.
- 30,000,000 more Americans will have access to the internet by the year 2000.
- The average attention span of Americans has been decreasing steadily since the advent of TV.

## Sales Evolution

Note the types of contacts that were around when traditional sales methods were cultivated. Picture the customer sitting around the radio at night listening to *AMOS & ANDY*. They went home from work at 5 p.m. every night while working the forty hour work week. They used a drafting board, a typewriter, and read the *Saturday Evening Post.* They used fountain pens, carbon paper, and had secretaries.

Don't hop on the traditional bandwagon. Adapt to the technology available to you now. Success lies in your ability to do this. The reasons are obvious. The world is changing at an ever faster pace and it is up to the professional to keep up. Avenues have been built that will change the world forever.

Alvin Toffler, in *FUTURE SHOCK*, described a society that changed so fast that it couldn't keep up with itself. This environment evolved as a result of a society that provided too much information.

Some say **_FUTURE SHOCK_** describes the business world today. If you look at it closely you might see the similarity. Recent statistics reveal that 1990's college graduates will change careers an average of eight times in their lifetime while 1950's graduates can count the number of jobs they had on one hand. Changes in accounting standards, tax codes, and business practices make the accountant a perpetually changing position. Windows users have already been through Windows 3.1, Windows 95, Windows 98, Office 97, and Office 2000 since 1994. Products in business are changing more quickly than ever before forcing network marketers to adjust or even change their selling styles.

Look closely at how all this change came about. If you look back as far as the TV, you would know that things have ended up exactly as they should have. That invention started moving communication from the mouth to the screen making us a visually stimulated society. Milton Berle could not have predicted that the 30 second commercial would start society in the direction of shorter messages and sound byte responses. This was a preview. It was also training. A entire generation was training to look at a TV screen and process information.

It continued with the advent of technology. Remember 25 years ago as the calculator became a standard? Many people probably ignored it at first looking at it as a luxury. It was something they didn't need. My parents used the slide ruler and went to the chalkboard in third grade. Just give a generation enough time to grow up and a little spending power and they will change things in a hurry. There was a generation using it, growing up on it, hoping that some day their teachers would finally say: "Sure, everyone can bring in their calculators for the final exam tomorrow." That day has come.

Remember Atari and Intellivision, Space Invaders and Galaga, Pac-man, and Breakout? Everyone should have known that bringing the arcade into the home was a preview of bringing the computer into the home. Those games evolved into DOS and then into Windows and let us thank Bill Gates for that. How about the movie "War Games?" The whole country was scared to death because they thought that a computer hacker from Seattle really could start WWIII.

Information Age selling is mastered using the computer. Sales people must understand how this tool will affect their jobs, present and future. Today's buyer's attention span is shorter. They are not so concerned about the relationship anymore. Today's buyer is concerned about the latest and greatest at the best value. You can argue that top management and high level buyers are not this way and I will agree with you. Remember though that they still are influenced by this style and are moving in this direction. Lexus commercials sell too, sometimes better than the Chevy S-10.

Today's customer expects perfection because a commercial is perfect. They expect you to look good because the model in a commercial looks good. They expect you to be short, sweet, and to the point because a commercial influenced them in only thirty seconds (How much time do you have?).

The trick seems to be short, stimulating, well-done exposures to a product. Make that a *lot* of exposures, too. That is the key. Get them at the right time, in their place, and with the good short message and you will sell a lot and you will feel guilty because you figured something out and don't work nearly as hard as others.

### Present Sales Environment

What changes should you pay attention to in today's sales environment?

What notices have been served?

Imagine a work regimen that would also allow you to teach yourself to learn. Imagine habits that not only make you successful in your everyday job but also prepare you for your next job and the next job after that.

The key in the 1990's is time management and how you use technology to make you more efficient. More and more employees lose their jobs each year because they are perceived as "old dogs" that can't learn new tricks.

Face it, network marketers don't have network marketing graduate school. We aren't sitting around the lunch table complaining about that masters sales class we are taking. We aren't planning what school we will attend to get our M.S.S. (Masters in Sales Strategy). What network marketers know are the methods that we are taught through experience.

In 1996 AT&T had one of the largest layoffs in corporate history when they laid off 40,000 people. The strangest part was that 60% of those laid off were white collar workers, many from the sales and marketing departments.

In the Information Age those methods will continue to change drastically.

Network marketers must think about this change and how they will adapt.

Have you thought about what your syllabus is going to look like? What are you prepared to do to make it exceptional?

This book is prepared to show how the computer has changed network marketing forever and how you can use it everyday. Log on and enjoy the ride!

# E-mail:
# The Arm that Reaches.

*"The best businessmen are the ones capable of influencing the most people."*
> *James Robinson (Mentor)*

*"The mark of highest originality lies in the ability to develop a familiar idea so fruitfully that it would seem no one else would ever had discovered so much to be hidden in it."*
> *Goethe*

*"I'd rather sit down and write a letter than call someone up. I hate the telephone."*
> *Henry Miller*

*"Everyone knows that sales is getting in via the point of least resistance."*
> *Don Robinson (President of Waddington JAYCARE's Injection Molding Division)*

Envision a business where the postman appears at the door at the exact moment you wanted to mail something and he delivers it to the recipient's mailbox within a second. In network marketing, this type of service would significantly improve prospecting and recruiting efficiency. It is easy to understand this when you look at a traditional cycle, especially during initial contact phases. (See figure 1.1)

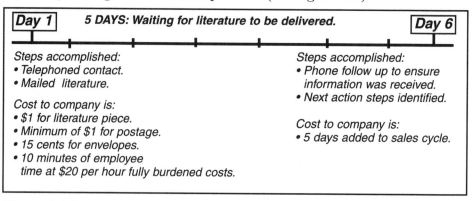

**Figure 1.1:** The above timeline of the initial steps in a network marketing cycle shows the inefficiency of traditional methods of getting information to a contact.

Figure 1.1, above, illustrates an example that costs $6.15 to send a literature piece to a new contact. Suppose that, in this example, the average network marketer sent literature to 150 new contacts annually. It would cost $922.50 each. Successful network marketers send out a lot more information than this. Are you starting to see the costs yet?

More importantly, mailing extends the cycle five days per new contact. Suppose the company in the example had 200 representatives to whom they supplied material. Using that scenario you note that this method adds 150,000 days (200 people x 150 new contacts x 5 days) to prospecting cycles annually. How valuable would it be for companies like this to be able to completely eliminate those days? Do you think executives would pay $10,000, $25,000 or even $50,000 for the opportunity to reduce prospecting cycle duration? What if they didn't have to pay? What if the service was free?

Well, that service already exists. It is e-mail.

E-mail is the messaging system on the internet. It is likely the most widely used computer tool.

One of the computer age's greatest benefits to network marketers is the incredible access to individuals. They now have instant and unlimited access to contacts.

Traditional network marketing methods include mailing lists to prospects. Mailings serve as methods of relaying company specific information valuable in prospecting. They continue to be a standard practice.

The incentive to improve on this method is the increase in competition in the information age. One hundred prospects need to become two hundred. This need mandates you to reach out to prospects more effectively.

How can you contact more prospects with less time and less money? A proactive approach is to use e-mail. This chapter will show you how to use e-mail and teach tricks to help you to continue influencing your prospects better and more often.

### How to Structure an E-mail Letter

You may have heard of the book <u>Selling to VITO</u> by Anthony Parinello. The subject of the book is how to get a meeting with the "Very Important Top Officer."

There is a chapter on headline statements in letters. These are sentences at the very top of the page that are usually in larger type and are meant to leap out of the page.

If you are attempting to get more distributors (and I hope you are because that is Fundamentals 101 in network marketing), then the headline statement is a good key to your letter. Be creative when writing it and try to cater the message to whom you are sending it, e.g. "Three ABC independent business owners that have been working part time with our group for three months are already making $5,000 monthly."

Send headline statement letters to prospects also. For example, if you are marketing to senior citizens, you can use a related statement, for example: "ABC's new vitamin was voted product of the year by nine out of ten fitness experts in a recent third party poll. It was rated as the most beneficial to senior citizens." This is a strong statement. The idea is no different than what is presented in Parinello's book. Keys to catering the letter to your audience may be discovered by asking yourself the following questions:

- How will the person receiving this e-mail benefit from my product?
- Will the person receiving this product be representing, using, or buying my product?
- What information from my research would strengthen my message?

- What can I add to this e-mail message that would capture this person's attention and keep it?
- What is the best time to forward the e-mail message?

The VITO approach is an excellent idea, but it is not the only way to communicate with the prospect. Follow the guidelines only as far as they apply and have confidence to try new ideas. It is only by that method that you can truly cultivate your talents and increase contacts.

## Including Information Via Hyperlinks

E-mail has many different faces. There are many different tools. There is one feature that could be one of the best tools in the e-mail suite, yet is only starting to be commonly used. It is called the hyperlink. Although, it sounds like a video game from the 1980's, it is a network marketer's information map for the prospect.

A hyperlink is an URL address to a website. It can be placed in messages. See the "How to Make a Hyperlink" Helpful Hint below.

## Helpful Hint: *How to Make a Hyperlink*

To make a hyperlink you must first type *http://*. That will trigger the e-mail to know you are typing in a link for the prospect to be able to access. (HTTP is an acronym for "Hypertext Transfer Protocol.")

Following HTTP you would type in the address:

http://www.networkmarketingproduct.com

The recipient knows it is something of interest because it is automatically highlighted in a different color by the browser. When the receiver reads their mail and clicks on the address they will go directly from the mail to the website (if they are connected to the internet at the time).

It is widely unknown that these exist and many of your recipients will not know how to use them. Note the hyperlink underneath the URL in the e-mail. Describe it by saying, "The above colored hyperlink will take you to a website that will allow you to learn more about our product. Just right click on the address in color. After browsing through the information please feel free to call me with any questions."

Hyperlinks are an extremely powerful way to get information to the prospect.

Some upline distributors have independent business owners in their group in other parts of the world. Keeping all levels informed can help their results. Forwarding e-mails with hyperlinks to information that keeps them enthusiastic, educated and, especially, productive will help everyone earn more money.

## *How to Hyperlink Specific Pages within a Website*

Being able to send specific page hyperlinks increases an e-mail's effectiveness because you can direct the prospect to any page on a website.

Don't get me wrong, sending a home page, such as http://www.abc.com, does has its benefits. The home page gives prospects a means to learn about your company. It is great as an opener, especially when you want your prospect to get the "30,000 foot view". However, in some correspondence, you may want to lead the prospect to more specific information.

If you send a prospect to your company's home page to see a specific product, they would have to search for it on the site. Sometimes, you may not want them to have to go through multiple pages just to find the information. That exercise would make it more painful. The prospect would probably tire of the page before reading the correct information.

Hyperlinks allow them to avoid that pain. The example below is from Northwestern Mutual Life Insurance Company:

Northwestern Mutual Life Insurance Home Page:
http://www.northwesternmutual.com
Northwestern Mutual Life Insurance Products:
http://www.northwesternmutual.com/planning/products/

The prospect has to search if you hyperlink the home page . The prospect goes directly to the desired page if you hyperlink the product's URL.  We will expand on this method in the next chapter.

## Hyperlinking from Your Company's Website vs. Sending Brochures or Materials

Many network marketing books explain how to use marketing material as a way to educate the prospect. Traditional prospecting methods use it as a step in the network marketing cycle. Although it is encouraged, it is not free to network marketers, as they usually have to pay for their marketing materials.

E-marketing tactics reduce the need for marketing prints. By using hyperlinks, the network marketer becomes more effective in educating his prospect, while spending less money.

Many of the materials typically mailed to the prospect can be hyperlinked. Note that a company's website consists of important marketing material, including:

- Product lists
- Company press releases
- Contact information
- Satellite locations

- Customer support
- Ordering information
- Partners
- Company financials

Review your company's website and you will find this information there. You can then note where it is located and begin to hyperlink it to your prospects instead of using mail. This is much more efficient than traditional methods.

## Hyperlinking References from the Web

John Steinbeck once said, "no one wants advice, just corroboration." How can you corroborate via the web?

Information hyperlinked to the prospect does not always have to be from your company's website. Take, for example, a situation where you are trying to convince a distribution prospect. Your potential distributor likes the opportunity, but feels he doesn't have the time. Instead of sending him information about your product over and over again, you can send him an objective website that supports your claim that ABC product makes money for its distributors. Find the site by searching for it and then hyperlink it over. When your potential distributor sees it is from an objective website you become more credible. Network marketing training has always taught that an objective reference is a powerful message. Sources of corroboration may be sites that speak of the advantages of your company or products. Examples are:

1. Customer sites that mention the advantages your products have brought their companies.
2. Independent research organizations that state the clear leadership of your product over competitor's products.
3. Other independent organization's testaments to your product's success.

After identifying sites, you can hyperlink them out to your contacts on a regular basis. An example of this type of site is found when searching the web . A researcher with a PhD and who has authored nine books did a study on Amway distributors and found that they are very successful personally, as well as in business. The site is a perfect example of testimony from an independent research organization. The address is: http://www.firedup.org/usa/letter2english.html. An Amway distributor can send this powerful site that is independent of Amway and is a great tool to use when selling.

---

### Helpful Hint: *Finding Reference Links*

The best way to find information on your company from independent sites is to use search engines. Go to a search engine and input your company's name:

"**ABC Inc.**". Many sites will probably be shown as a result of this search.

You can look at some of the titles and see if the descriptions are close enough to warrant browsing through the results. However, you may find that you have to narrow your search further.

Try to be more specific in searching sections, e.g. "**Positive information**". From that point forward you will probably find some sites attesting to your product's value.

If you want general company information, try the company name. Then try words like "leader," "performance," "rated," or "compared" in searching these results. If you use a little common sense, chances are you will be able to find something beneficial to your cause that you can attach as a link.

You will find more on searching in chapter three.

---

### Sending E-mail Before Meetings

A network marketer's first meeting with a prospect is crucial and it is important to be prepared. I remember when I first started selling. I would call for a meeting with a new prospect and, many times, as salespeople have to do, I would settle for a shorter than desired meeting so as to fit it into the prospect's schedule.

I would go to the meeting loaded for bear. I was prepared to talk about goals, objectives, and next steps. All the key steps to advancements were on my agenda. It was funny, though, how long it took me to notice that these meetings were not as effective as I'd like them to be. I'd be getting questions from the prospects that were extremely basic:

"What is the name of your company again?"

"How long have you been in business?"

"What is it, exactly, that you sell?"

Many minutes were wasted. Half hour meetings became ten minutes. Ten minutes were not enough to influence all of the people I needed to make money. Every network marketer has experienced the frustration of the prospect that didn't have enough time to read the mail:

NETWORK MARKETER: "Did you have a chance to read the brochure I sent to you?"

PROSPECT: "Oh yes, I think I received the literature. Oh, where did I put that? Oh, well. I might have received it but didn't have any time to page through it. Could you please give me the reader's digest version of what you sent me?"

Why weren't they reading what I had sent? Those slicks cost a dollar each. Don't they know it is expensive to print up those incredibly beautiful brochures? How about postage? It cost $6 to send those second day air just so they would have enough time to read it. Where is the consideration? Where is the humanity? Well, I finally figured out where their time was going instead of reading my material. They were checking their e-mail.

A good practice is to send products or services information from your website via hyperlinks before going to meetings. You can include financing, services, products, or a company overview. It is probable that your company website contains information that relates to your discussion.

The advantages of sending something via e-mail versus regular mail:

1. <u>Most people check e-mail daily.</u> Everyone has signals on their computer that will immediately notify them that they have received a message.   Chances are that when they hear that sound they will turn around and immediately read your e-mail .

2. <u>People are swamped with junk mail at home and at work.</u> Sending material in the mail only adds to the information pile.   People are accustomed to throwing things of disinterest into the trashcan.

3. <u>Losing an e-mail is a lot harder than losing a brochure.</u>  Even if a prospect has the best intentions, many brochures find their way into the trashcan via the process of elimination. A person doing housecleaning in the office sometimes will throw away anything that makes clutter, and that includes your brochure!

4. <u>Hyperlinks are novelties.</u> People are enjoying the web and the information gathered from it. The web is more dynamic than reading. People are comfortable processing information from a picture tube.

5. <u>A hyperlink takes your prospect directly to the information you think is most interesting.</u> A website is like an electronic brochure with different pages. A hyperlink allows you to send a prospect directly to a page in that brochure. If you are trying to be specific in your message, hyperlinks are the best way to do it without forcing your prospect to have to search from the home page.

6. <u>Less expense.</u>  Postage and printing are expensive.  Setting up a website is free and costs as little as $25 per month to host. Hyperlinking your website is just as good, if not better, than the brochure.

Envision situations where a potential new independent business owner has expressed sincere interest. Before the next meeting you could send information specific to a feature of the opportunity you know might excite them.

You can write:

> Dear Opportunity Seeker,
>
> After our meeting the other night I was glad to learn of your excitement. The hyperlinks below will direct you to information that will get you even more fired up about this lifetime opportunity. After you review them, please hit the third hyperlink to review our company.
>
> http://www.company.com/products/ecommerce.html
> http://www.company.com/success/diamonds.html
> http://www.company.com/about/
>
> I look forward to our next meeting on Saturday.
>
> Yours in success,
>
> Gerry Robinson

This method, compared to sending brochures, is much more efficient. It is less cumbersome to the prospect, readily accessible to them, easy to retain without clogging up their desk, fun for them to explore, and inexpensive for you to send.

## Signatures

E-mail signatures are previously made salutations that can attach to any new message you compose. The signature function saves time by automatically attaching all of your contact information to an outgoing e-mail. Suggestions of things to include in the signature are:

- Name
- Address
- Phone numbers (Mobile, Office, Pager, and Fax)
- Product Web Site URL (for all of your friends to see what you sell)
- Website access number for e-commerce network marketers where the buyer uses the distributor's code in order to purchase. This has also been successful because it intrigues people to inquire about an IBO's business, thus increasing the number of contacts that may become downlines.

For an example see figure 1.2.

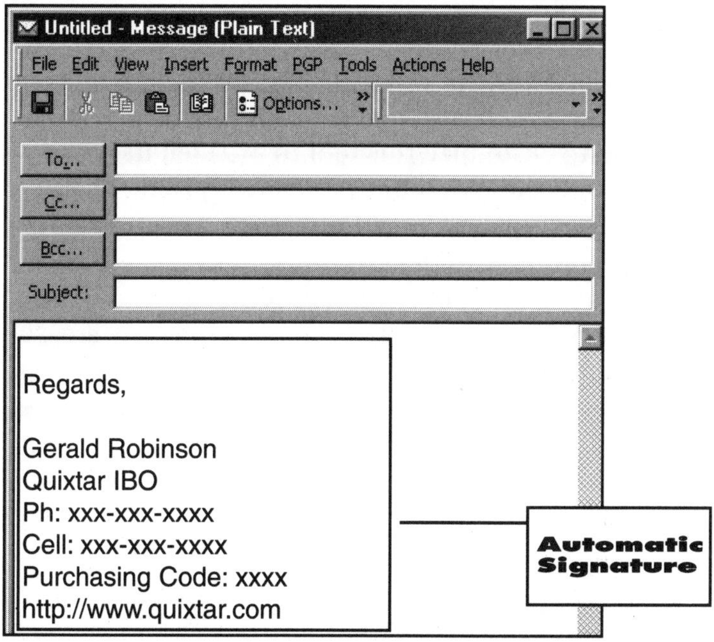

**Figure 1.2:** *Signature* containing contact information. This automatically attaches to new messages when you configure it correctly. The above new window appears with the signature already contained.

## Helpful Hint: *Creating Signatures*

Creating *signatures* in **Microsoft Outlook** is easy. Create them using the following menu picks:

1. Tools
2. Options
3. Mail Format
4. Signature Picker (found at bottom of window)

Create *signatures* in **Netscape Communicator** using the following menu picks:

1. Edit
2. Preferences
3. Identity (On file tree on the left of the window)
4. Edit Card

(***Netscape Communicator*** only allows for one *signature* card.)

## Using Signatures to Quickly Make E-mails (in Outlook 98 only)

*Signatures* can be used for much more than contact information. You can manually insert *signatures* into a new message. This capability allows you to customize this tool to broaden its use. An example is when you want to send hyperlinks containing product specific information.

Suppose, while on a phone call with a contact, you told them you were going to send information regarding Product X via e-mail. By creating a standard information request *signature* you can type an entire letter in very few menu picks. Those menu picks are Insert, Signature, and Product X Information request. (See figures 1.3 and 1.4).

Getting back to our Amway example, we note that a distributor can create *signatures* for the most popular products. When that distributor wants to send product specific information it becomes as simple as twelve keystrokes.

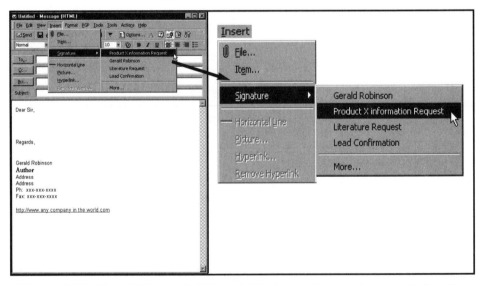

**Figure 1.3** (left) and **Figure 1.4** (above): Window and menus for manually inserting a *signature*. This can be used for contact information requests on your products and company.

What results when you insert the *signature* in figure 1.4 into an e-mail is shown in figure 1.5.

24

| To... | |
| Cc... | |
| Bcc... | |
| Subject: | |

Dear Sir,

Per our discussion, attached find the information regarding Product X. Please browse the below links to read more about it:

http://www.anycompany.com/products/X.html
http://www.anycompany.com/training/productx.html

Also this link will tell you more about our company:

http://www.anycompany.com/company/overview.html

Please call with any questions.

Regards,

**Inserted in three menu picks.**

Gerald Robinson
**Author**
Address
Address
Ph: xxx-xxx-xxxx
Fax: xxx-xxx-xxxx

**Inserted automatically when you opened the window.**

**Figure 1.5:** A *signature* containing an information request letter. This can be manually inserted into a message to save time. This is significant when used correctly. This message was completed in 12 keystrokes. Notice the hyperlink to specific product information on the website.

## E-mail PowerPoint Presentations as Attachments

Imagine a prospect 20 years ago going to a briefing where the presentation had graphics, spinning words, or even more than one page. The prospect would have fallen off their chair and thought the presenter spent $5,000 and too much time. In the 1990's, these people see this type of presentation every day. **Excel, Word, PowerPoint,** and **Publisher** have taken presentations to new artistic heights.

Part of learning the effectiveness of the computer is to learn when and how to apply your information. Many network marketing books recommend printing direct mailers for campaigns. **PowerPoint** can replace this expensive step in the process. E-mail allows you to send effective **PowerPoint** presentations out to the prospect without cost and with little difficulty, thus allowing you to use it often.

All of the presentations in your files can be used at any time.

**PowerPoint** presentations are very effective. This is a strong tool that can be used as much in e-mail as it can be in the conference room. As you create more presentations it is a good idea to start thinking of instances where you would want to send the information to more contacts. Start creating files with this intention. Look back over your presentations and review the effective ones before you read the next sections.

Many network marketers know how to use **PowerPoint**. However, animating slides using Custom Animation is largely unknown.

By animating slides you create a show for the prospect. These shows can be sent to them via e-mail as attachments. They transfer and open up immediately into a show after the prospect clicks it. You can narrate for more effective presentations. (Please note: As of the printing of this book, many e-mail recipients still do not have high speed internet access. So, keep the narration short so you do not keep your contact waiting by the computer while your large files download).

---

## Helpful Hint: *Animating Objects in PowerPoint for a Presentation*

To animate objects in **PowerPoint** you must do the following:

1. While you create your presentation, highlight the object (e.g. text box) you would like to animate.
2. Right click and select Custom Animation.
3. You will have a choice of Timing, Effects, Chart Effects, and Play Settings.
4. The Effects menu pick allows you to choose an animation such as *appear*, or flying the object in from the left of the screen, box-in, or box-out. Whatever you choose should help you make a point in a presentation.
5. Timing coordinates in what order the objects will be presented. This is important. You must figure out the order of your discussion before setting the timings. Introduce the objects into the **PowerPoint** show as you would introduce subjects into your presentation. This allows for a logical flow and a more effective presentation.

26

**Figure 1.6 (left) and Figure 1.7 (right):** Custom Animation of **PowerPoint** objects for a presentation.

---

**Helpful Hint:** *Saving PowerPoint as a Show*

To save a **PowerPoint** presentation so that it will automatically engage in *View Show* from the prospect's e-mail you must do the following:

1. Save the file as a standard **PowerPoint** presentation (.ppt).

2. After saving it the first time open it and click File and then Save As.

3. Then save the file as a show (.pps). Please note figure 1.8.

4. Attach the show to your e-mail.

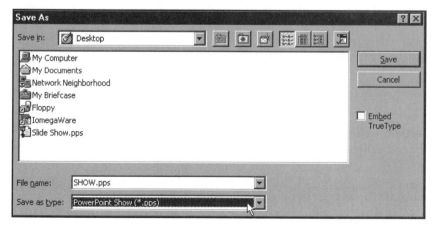

**Figure 1.8:** Saving a **PowerPoint** presentation as a show for automatic viewing.

27

When the prospect clicks to open the file it will automatically go into viewing mode.

If you would like to send the file and make absolutely sure your prospect can't change it, you can buy programs like Lotus Screen Cam (http://www.lotus.com) and download them from the internet. They can record the **PowerPoint** show as a view only file. Please note the prospect must have a viewer program for this. However, many of these are free from the web and probably will be a computer standard within a short time. You can even send a free viewer from this program to the contact.

---

## How to Find Your Prospect's E-mail Address

There are certain ways to obtain the e-mail address of people you are trying to contact. Take a look at the following scenario:

You are calling into ABC Inc. and you get a receptionist on the line. This call is to contact someone in the financial department to ask some questions related to the information you found on the web. You ask the secretary if you can speak with the director of budgeting and finance. After what seems to be an impossibly short time checking whether she is in at the moment, the secretary gets back on the line and says: "Miss Budget is not in right now. Can I forward you to her voice mail?" You answer "yes" knowing that some contact is a minor victory. You are transferred and hear the greeting: "You have reached Gretchen Budget of ABC Inc. I am either not at my desk or on the other line. Please leave a message and I will get back to you as soon as I can."

Aside from leaving a message, what can you take out of this failed attempt to contact Gretchen Budget?

First, you can call back and ask for her e-mail address. If whomever you contact doesn't give you the information then follow the next step.

Typically, e-mail addresses for people are name driven. For example, my e-mail address is grobinson@company.com. Can you assume that this might be the case for your contact? Chances are her address is gbudget@abc.com. Another possibility is her address may be gretchen.budget@abc.com. Ninety-five percent of the time it will be one of these two formats.

When you get a message rejection (see Helpful Hint that defines message rejection) try the next steps:

**Company directories:** Employee directories are a great resource. They are often available on company websites. When marketing to IBM for example, you will find on their homepage an icon named "Contacting IBM". When you click on that icon you find **"Look up the e-mail address for an IBM employee."** Jackpot! Now whenever you call into this company and get a name that could be important all you have to do is go to this website and look up their name.

**Call and ask for the contact's e-mail address from a receptionist or secretary:** This is the easiest way to get the e-mail address. Practice this tactic. Here is an example of what you might say: "Yes, hello, this is Gerry and I was supposed to e-mail some information to Gretchen but I seem to have lost her e-mail address. It is no wonder why Federal Express turned down my application for delivery man. Can you do me a favor and tell me her e-mail address again?" I'll bet she gives it to you. But if she says she is not allowed then try another tactic.

**Ask the receptionist or secretary for their e-mail address and ask if they can forward a letter to your contact:** The receptionist will probably give you their e-mail address. "..........Well, my e-mail is Jane.Doe@ABC.com." Then you ask Jane what the correct spelling of Miss Budget's name is for your letter. Little does Jane know, but she just gave you your contact's e-mail address. Plug in the answers to your questions. If Jane's e-mail is FirstName.LastName@company.com then Gretchen's must be Gretchen.Budget@ABC.com.

If you're marketing to households and not to corporations then the way to find your contact's e-mail address is easy. All you have to do is go to one of the "Find an e-mail" search engines on the web. There is no guarantee with these as they often times are out of date or don't register your prospect's address. However, there are some reliable engines out there and once you find your favorites you should continually go back to them and use them. Many times you'll find that for which you are looking.

## Helpful Hint: *Message Rejection Notices*

Try and send an e-mail if you aren't sure  that you have the correct address. If you guessed wrong (which won't be the case often with the mentioned methods) your e-mail will be returned with a message back:

**Mail Delivery Subsystem ...Returned Mail Address Unknown.**

After each returned message follow the next step listed in this book. Chances are you will get to your contact.

## *Address Book*

The address book is your personal library of e-mail addresses. You can use this feature to communicate with large numbers of contacts. In this tool, you can create lists that contain specific prospects, customers, professionals, and company partners.  You can then send them e-mails with information that is helpful to your prospecting campaign.

Address book groups should, in addition to the e-mail address, include vital information like organization name, phone number, and location.

The lists can contain many addresses. It saves you time by streamlining the process and making addressing many people a one step function. It is clearly a key to those who want to market via the web.

## Helpful Hint: *Mailing Lists*

Creating prospect and customer e-mail mailing lists is easy.  When creating them in your address book, consider the following:

1. Construct mailing groups based on strategic information.  An example is to have multiple mailing lists:

 • **Independent Business Owner Prospects (which can include):**
   - Relatives.
   - Neighbors.
   - Current Friends.
   - Old Friends.
   - School Friends.
   - Work Associates.

- Members of groups you belong to such as associations, church groups, clubs, sports, and community groups.
- Fellow commuters.
- Merchant or store clerks where you shop.
- People who have services that you use such as doctors and dentists.
- Acquaintances.
- Referrals.

- **Distributors.**
- **Customers.**
- **Corporate Contacts**

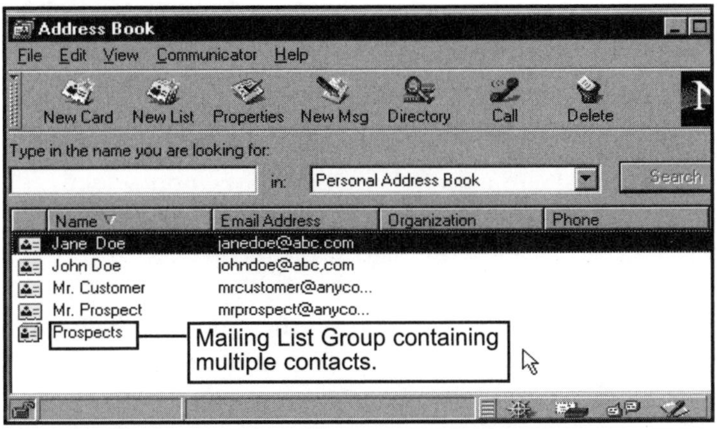

*Figure 1.9: Netscape Communicator's* Address Book.

2. If you want to keep contacts from seeing the others to whom you send a message send the e-mail to yourself and Blind Carbon Copy (BCC:) the mailing group. This is an addressing feature (like TO: and CC:) in every major e-mail manager (such as **Outlook** and *Netscape Communicator*).This ensures no one will see the others who receive the message. This is important when sending messages to multiple distributor prospects.

## *Adding to the Address Book*

Another feature to look for in your address book is the ability to add names to it from a message. Key functionality in name referencing includes:

- The browser should be capable of adding names, by clicking on them, directly to the address book from the *signature* bar on an incoming message.
- Ensure that your address book allows you to create address groups so that you can send out mass mailings by group name such as **Prospects, Customers, and Distributors** (please see Figure 1.9).
- The ability should exist to file e-mail addresses by contact names (like first name or nickname). This will allow you to input the recipient's name into the address bar and the address associated with that name will appear. This saves you from having to go to the address book and waste time searching. For example: John Smith's e-mail address is John_Smith@abc.com. Instead of inputting the entire address every time you send a message, you can simply type "JOHN S" and the browser should automatically input John Smith@abc.com. (For **Microsoft Outlook** simply type the first few letters of the name of the addressee and select CTRL K).

## E-mail Filters

Filters automatically file e-mails as they arrive. This is a great advantage for the network marketer who sends and receives a lot of e-mail. Filters work by signaling the browser via words in an arriving message. The trigger word can be located in the address, subject, date, body, or priority.

A high priority message is an example of where the network marketer can create filters to aid in organizational efficiency. Network marketers receive many e-mails daily. Time constraints prohibit them from reading all new e-mail. However, many are high priority. This is where a filter could be useful.

Use filters to file any mail that contains trigger words relating to the high priority subject or person. These can include e-mail from:

- Top distributors sorted by their e-mail address.
- Any network marketing related message filtered by product name.
- Key prospects or customers.

Create named folders where you can file the high priority messages. This system will identify important messages and file them in a place where you can view them effortlessly. You can read the low priority e-mails later when you have more time.

### Helpful Hint: *Creating New Folders in Your Inbox*

Menu Picks are:

| Microsoft Outlook | Netscape Communicator |
|---|---|
| 1. File | 1. File |
| 2. New | 2. New Folder |
| 3. Folder | |

Note: Make sure the new folder is created as a sub-folder to your choice file (such as inbox).

### Helpful Hint: *Creating Mail Filters*

Creating mail filters within *Netscape Communicator* is simple. Go to the Edit menu and scale down to Mail Filters. When you get to Mail Filters you will find three icons. Pick the New icon and start creating (See figure 1.10).

You will find that you can sort in a variety of ways and use multiple combinations to sort, such as sender, subject, body, date, and priority.

**Filter Rules**

Filter name: ABC Project

| If the | body | of the message | contains | ABC |
| and the | sender | of the message | contains | abc.com |
| and the | subject | of the message | contains | ABC Project |

More    Fewer

then Move to folder    ABC Project

Description: Filter for sorting messages coming into my mail box on this urgent project .

Filter is: ○ Off ● On    OK    Cancel    Help

*Figure 1.10: Netscape Communicator* filtering e-mails based on multiple criteria.

The ways to differentiate the sorting objects vary and include: contain, doesn't contain, is, isn't, begins with, and ends with.

A filter can also file messages in the trash. An example of where this is advantageous is if you are consistently barraged with e-mail from a source in spite of your wish to not receive their messages. You can file any e-mail that comes from that source into trashcan so you never have to read them. See figure 1.11 for an example.

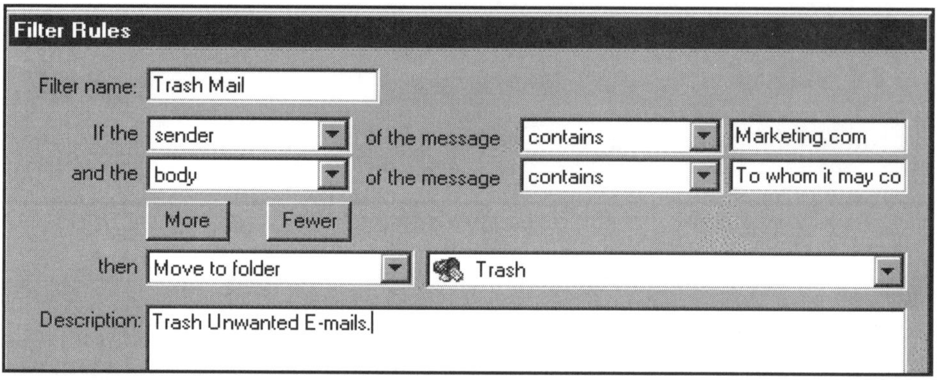

*Figure 1.11: Netscape Communicator* filtering e-mail to Trash Can file.

**Microsoft's** version of filters is in **Outlook** which is integrated with **Explorer**. To enable filters within **Outlook** just go to Organize on the menu bar (see figure 1.12).

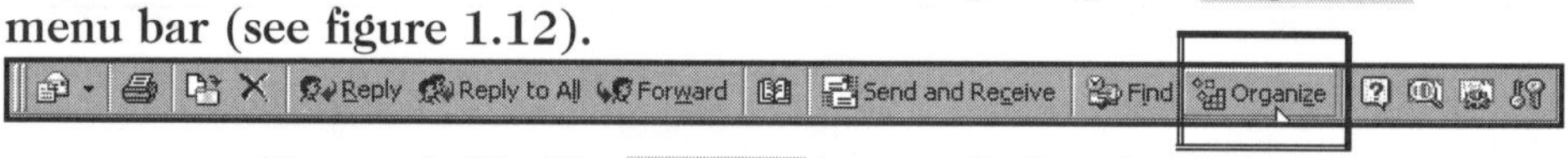

*Figure 1.12:* The Organize icon on **Outlook's** title bar.

Select Rules Wizard.... (figure 1.13) and you will find a very easy menu that will walk you through the steps.

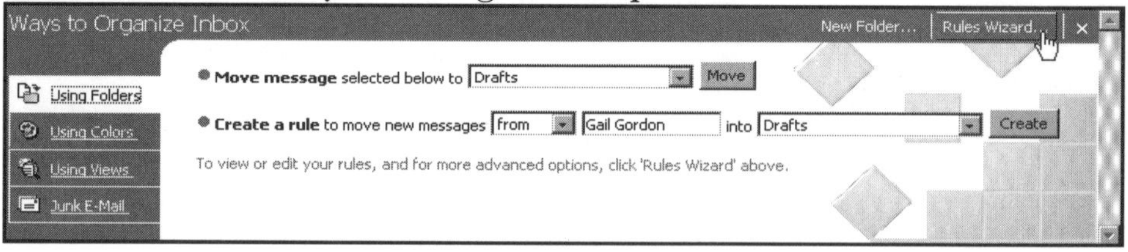

*Figure 1.13:* **Microsoft Outlook's** filtering menu.

### Responding to E-mail While You're Away at a Meeting or on Vacation

Network marketers, when on vacation or out of the office, are often faced with the dilemma of how to notify a contact that they are unavailable to respond to their e-mail. To solve this problem, they can configure their mail account to deliver a responding message whenever an e-mail is received (See the Helpful Hint "Setting up Out-of-the-Office Replies" to learn how to set these up). To do this, you must set up a message that tells the sender that they shouldn't expect an immediate response and specify your return date. You can also tell the sender to call a specific number in an emergency, or to contact someone else who can support his or her request in your absence. Many service providers may not offer this to residential users. Check with your provider for how to get this service.

## Helpful Hint: *Setting up Out-of-the-Office Replies*

**Internet Explorer** provides this functionality in **Outlook.** Select Tools and then scale down and select Out of Office Assistant... and follow the directions. See figures 1.14 and 1.15.

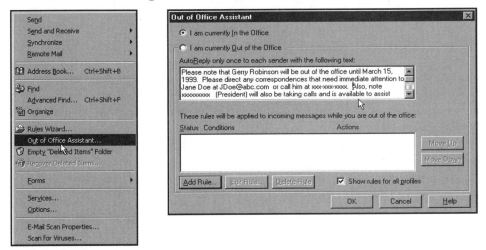

***Figure 1.14*** (left) and ***Figure 1.15*** (right): **Microsoft Outlook's** Out of Office automated messenger menu picks and input screen.

***Netscape Communicator*** provides this functionality under the Edit menu at Manage Mail Account. Servers will have varying setups; however, most organizations will have a place to manage your mail account.

## Summary

This chapter described how to use e-mail as an effective way to send information to many prospects with little  effort and no cost.

It starts by giving suggestions on how you can construct an e-mail letter that would get attention. Next it explains hyperlinks and attachments in detail as excellent ways to quickly include specific information in e-mails. Reference links are noted, as is the importance of looking for websites that are unrelated to your company but that can serve as a testament to your product. These can be hyperlinked in e-mail messages. *Signatures* are covered to show the power of automating e-mail systems and including hyperlinks.  In our example, a three-paragraph e-mail was composed in 12 keystrokes. Tips are provided on how to find a prospect's e-mail address if you don't have it.

PowerPoint presentations are covered in this chapter because of their effectiveness as attachments in e-mails. Saving these presentations as shows and animating them for delivery via e-mail are explained because of their importance in replacing expensive direct mailings.

Finally, time saving tactics such as  e-mail filtering for automatic mail organization, setting up automatic replies to e-mails sent to you while you are out of the office, and address book pointers for sending out mass e-mailings are detailed.

E-mail is normally an effective way to communicate to your prospects. However, by applying the tactics described in this chapter you become even more efficient. One of the cornerstones of success is time management. E-mail can help.

# 2

# Browser Power!

*"O, what a brave thing it is, in every case and circumstance of a matter, to be thoroughly well informed."*
   *Rabelais*

*"The man who is too old to learn was probably always too old to learn."*
   *Henry S. Haskins*

*"Who forces time is pushed back by time; who yields to time finds time on his side.*
   *THE TALMUD*

*"Ordinary people merely think how they shall spend their time; a man of talent tries to use it."*
   *Arthur Schopenhauer*

Imagine James Bond having a supercharged 350 horsepower, luxury, cherry red, BMW fully equipped with missiles, machines guns, and turbo boosters. That is a lot of power at his fingertips. He could defeat a small country with that vehicle.

Now, imagine him being in a small fire fight and needing to shoot a missile from his BMW. He goes to fire and he can't figure out the system menu, or even worse, he looks at the control panel and realizes it doesn't contain a button to shoot the missile.

He would be dead in that situation, wouldn't he? He would have lost and his competitor would have won.

That same death happens every day to the network marketer with the wrong internet browser. At the network marketer's fingertips is the "James Bond Cherry Red BMW" of research and prospecting, which is the internet. By utilizing the wrong browser, network marketers ensure they will not be able to access valuable information.

Don't let yourself fall into that trap.

The purpose of this chapter is to inform you of the features that browsers must have and how they can help improve your efficiency.

## Where the Browser Can Help

The main ways the browser can help the network marketer are:

- Copying and pasting: informing prospects and customers efficiently.
- Sitemarking: saving and organizing valuable websites.
- Browsing the web: researching and prospecting.
- Using information from the web in presentations and documents.

## Copy and Paste

"Plagiarism is the sincerest form of flattery" is a pearl of wisdom repeated throughout the ages by the many that have seen the value in other's works. It is true to an extent and network marketers see it on every side. They see it when another network marketer's methods are so effective that upline distributors stand him or her in front of the room to teach it to them. They see it when their companies release bulletins on tactics perfected in the field by other network marketers.

Using the computer in the network marketing process is no different.

Copying and pasting is the most powerful function a browser can offer. Some of the features available are:

- Send product specific information in less than 5 seconds to up to 99 people using hyperlinks and address books.
- Import pictures from the web for use in presentations.
- Copy sections of web pages to letters you are mailing.
- Paste material into **PowerPoint** presentations, documents, spreadsheets, new and reply-to messages, and schedulers.

### Copying Links

It is not necessary to manually type a long website into a document or e-mail. There is an easier way to create a hyperlink. Simply copy it by following the "How to Copy a Website Address..." Helpful Hint in this chapter.

---

## Helpful Hint: *How to Copy a Website Address from the Title Bar*

To copy a site you are visiting:

- Move the pointer so that it is directly on the address in the address bar (see figure 2.1).
- Left click once so that the address is highlighted.
- Go to the Edit menu and select Copy.
- Go to the program into which you would like to paste such as **Word, Excel, PowerPoint,** e-mail, etc.
- Select Paste and it will be inserted. Please note, that no matter how long the address is, this function will paste it.

**Figure 2.1:** Address bar with address highlighted for copying into another program. This is great for creating hyperlinks quickly in e-mails.

---

This feature can be helpful when you want to send a hyperlink in an e-mail. Instead of manually typing it into the mail message all you have to do is copy it from the address bar. It does not matter how long the address is.

## Use Material from Websites in Presentations and to Address Quotes & Letters

I was required in one job to make my own quotations. I utilized **Excel** to make the quotes. At the time, I had been acquiring customer and prospect addresses from people search engines on the web. For months, I manually typed the five and six line addresses into the documents.

One day I was thinking of how awesome it would be to copy the mailing addresses directly from the web and paste them into my documents so I wouldn't have to manually type. I fiddled around with the idea and found out how to do this. The way to copy website text is to highlight the words via click and drag and Copy / Paste it to the program you are using. You should also use this feature for information from your own company's web address book.

The ability to copy web text to other programs in **Microsoft Office** makes Copy / Paste an incredibly powerful tool. There are many examples where copying from the web will improve your efficiency:

- Addressing documents.
- Transferring information into your personal contact book (such as **Outlook**) including:
  - Address, phone and contact information.
- Relevant information found in internet searches.
- Material from websites that can be effective in presentations to your prospect.
- E-mail addresses.
- Research for presentations.

## Copying E-mail Addresses

How many times have you had to manually type an e-mail address from another program into an outgoing message's address bar? Probably many times if you use the e-mail search engines on the web. Manually typing these addresses is no longer necessary with <u>C</u>opy & <u>P</u>aste. To copy an e-mail address:

- Highlight the address (it doesn't matter where you are highlighting. It could be an address from a website, **Word**, **PowerPoint**, **Excel**, e-mail, etc.), e.g. grobinson@ABC.com
- Select <u>E</u>dit.
- Select <u>C</u>opy.
- Go to the address bar of your new message.
- Select <u>E</u>dit.
- Select <u>P</u>aste.

## *A Picture is Worth a Thousand Words*

Imagine presenting an awesome **PowerPoint** slide show complete with statistics, graphs, metrics, and valuable information to a prospect. The presentation focuses on a product that can make an impact. Wouldn't it be more effective to include a visual reference of the product in your presentation? Would a cover page with your corporate logo help?

The web is a source for pictures that can enhance the quality of your presentations. You can obtain them using the save function. Using pictures from the web is so easy and helpful it is hard to believe it isn't more widely known.

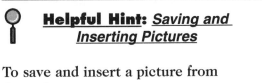

**Helpful Hint:** *Saving and Inserting Pictures*

To save and insert a picture from the web:
- Move the pointer on to the picture that you would like to copy.
- Right click your mouse.
- Select Save Image As.
- Go to the file in which you want to save the image and name the picture.

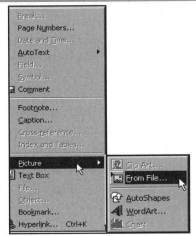

*Figure 2.2:* Menu picks for inserting a picture.

**41**

- Go to the program into which you are inserting.
- Select Insert and then select Picture .
- Select From File and go to the file you saved the image in and select the saved image.

---

### Helpful Hint: *Where to Find Good Pictures*

Ideal websites to find good pictures are:

1. Prospect and customers websites.

2. Competitor websites.

3. Search engine query results listing websites related to your product.

---

### Helpful Hint: *Website Text Copy/Paste Example*

Go to any website. Look for the corporate office address. Place your pointer at the first letter of the first word until it appears as an $(I)$ . At the first letter, click your left mouse button and hold while you drag the pointer on the words you want to copy. End the click and drag at the last letter of the last word you want to copy.

At this point, go to the Edit  menu and select Copy. Then go to any other Windows program and select Paste. What will be pasted is the text from the website. Once again, you will see awesome time savings.

---

### *Sitemarking*

Sitemarking a website is the act of saving it in a folder so that you can revisit it in the future. Sitemarking is an easy step and doesn't take much time. The advantages of sitemarking are:

- Sites can be accessed frequently without typing the website address.
- Most marked sites are referenced by title.
- Research and prospecting becomes an organized function.

The names for sitemarking used by ***Netscape Communicator*** and **Explorer** are different. They are Bookmarking and Favorites (see figures 2.3 and 2.4), respectively.

**42**

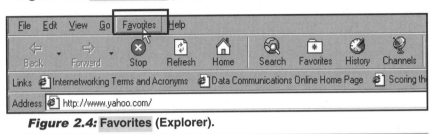

*Figure 2.3:* Bookmarking *(Communicator).*

*Figure 2.4:* Favorites (Explorer).

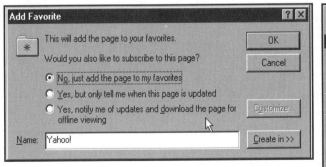

**Helpful Hint:** *Menu Picks to Create Sitemark Files in Explorer and Netscape Communicator*

### Explorer

1. Favorites
2. Add to   Favorites
3. Create In >>
4. New Folder

### Communicator

1. Communicator
2. Bookmarks
3. Edit Bookmarks
4. File/New Folder

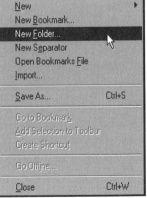

*Figure 2.5* (left) and *Figure 2.6* (right): Adding sitemark folders to **Explorer** and **Communicator.**

43

## Naming Sitemark Files

Naming files in a browser's sitemarks manager is a more advanced way of using this tool. The way you file sitemarks will greatly affect how efficient you are while communicating with your downlines, prospects and customers.

Let me give you an example:

Suppose you sell vitamins and your company's website has every product listed on separate pages. Some products may be suitable for young children and others for senior citizens. You can create a sitemark file named "Children's Vitamins" and another named "Vitamins for Senior Citizens." You can sitemark the products in the appropriate files, and as you will see later in the chapter, you can copy and paste them as hyperlinks into e-mails.

This process allows you to group related sites together in the same file. You can send entire files as hyperlinks to anyone via an e-mail in seconds.

## Deciding What to Sitemark

The five questions below should be asked before you sitemark a website:
1. Is the information on this site valuable to my everyday activities?

2. Does this information change often enough to warrant frequent visits?

3. How could I use this site if I were to visit it often?

4. Will I be sending this site via hyperlinks to prospects or customers? (Pages like customer metrics, independent organization recommendations, etc.)

5. Would the information on this page answer frequently asked questions by my customer?

Using these five questions, you begin to assemble a list of sitemarks that become very beneficial. Also, there are sites that are common sitemarks. As a rule of thumb you should be on the lookout for sites that are listed in this section. Even if you mark and file them later you will have a head start versus 90% of your peers.

The sites are:

- Your company's product's websites.
- Product user group sites.
- Competitor's sites.
- People search engines.
- Online phone books.
- Map websites.
- Travel planning websites.
- Your company's phone, address, and e-mail address book page.
- Customer, prospect, and associate company's address books on the web where you can search out a contact's e-mail, phone and address.
- Prospecting sites such as company financial sites, industry magazine sites and business news links.

---

## Helpful Hint: *Organizing Sitemarks*

Just like account files, sitemarks are information maps that must be kept organized. Organizing them will enable you to use them effectively. When organizing sitemarks, figure out how the information on each site applies to your network marketing process and create an appropriately named file in the sitemarks manager. Examples of

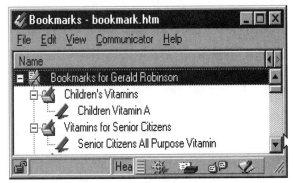

**Figure 2.7: Netscape Communicator** bookmark files named to reference product sites quickly.

files can be prospects and/or customers (divided by product or market), company partners, company products, training, press releases, and other miscellaneous information.

See figure 2.7 for an example. Senior citizen and children's vitamin sites may be in files named "Vitamins for Senior Citizens" and "Children's Vitamins". When you want to send these sites via hyperlinks, you can go to the appropriate file and copy and paste it to the e-mail message.

## Copying Sitemark Files into E-mail to Save Time (in Netscape Communicator only)

You can send an entire sitemark file containing valuable information on a particular product or service by copying that sitemark file from the sitemark manager and pasting it into your e-mail message.

Figure 2.8 illustrates what will result. The file becomes hyperlinks when pasted. Entire sitemark files can be transferred to e-mails in one step. By pasting the files as hyperlinks, you create information maps for the contact that improve your chances of success.

This feature is a great time saver for the network marketer. It replaces outdated methods such as faxes, brochures, and marketing material that has to be gathered, packaged, and sent. You begin to use your website to reach out to your customer, instead of only relying on it to draw them in.

Include messages in the file names such as: "Below find the information you requested." When you paste, the file name will appear as a message to the customer and the files will appear as hyperlinks.

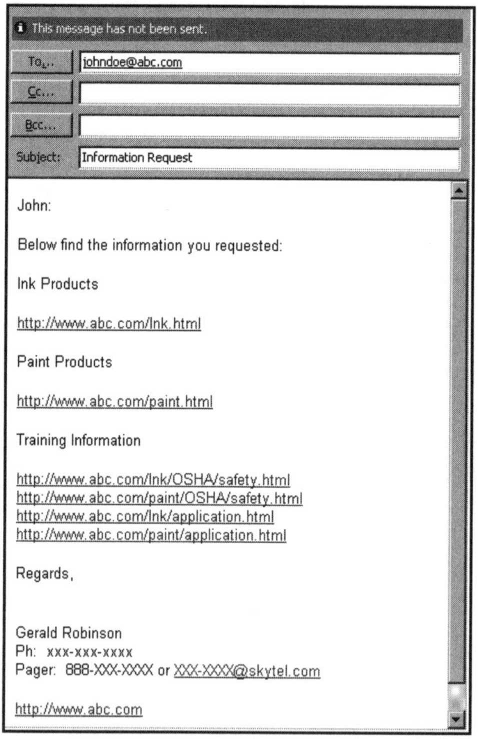

**Figure 2.8:** Message containing copied sitemark files that become hyperlinks when pasted from sitemarks into e-mail.

You should sitemark pages from your own website. Include pages like products, services, and financing information. File these sites within the Bookmarks/Favorites manager under file folders with names fitting their description (*Products, Leases,* etc.).

Companies that include information on their website that is commonly sent out as sales material enable their network marketers to replace time consuming methods of the past. This also saves the company and network marketers money in printing, material and postage costs.

Research your company's website and determine the information you can use as hyperlinks instead of mailing materials. It will change the way you market!

---

## Helpful Hint: *Sitemark Managers*

*Netscape Communicator* sitemarks manager can be located by:

1. Selecting Bookmarks on the browser toolbar.
2. Select Edit Bookmarks...
3. At this point you are in the manager.

**Internet Explorer** sitemarks manager can be located by:

1. Selecting Favorites on the browser toolbar.
2. Select Organize Favorites...
3. At this point you are in the manager.

---

### Making Hyperlink Summary Sheets

A Hyperlink Summary Sheet is a list of website addresses that you can copy to e-mail. They include websites that contain valuable information that a network marketer believes a prospect should know to improve the chances of a sale. Included with the URL's are descriptions of the sites. These lists are made so that a network marketer can send many of these quickly for mass marketing. This is done by copying and pasting to e-mail messages.

These sheets are an alternative to pasting sitemark files. They are used when a more detailed description is needed. Sitemark files will only include the URL and file name when pasted. Hyperlink Summary Sheets include as much description as desired.

Make multiple pages in your list. Include pages from your own website, independent websites, competitor's websites, and industry specific websites. You can have categories such as financials, products, revenues, customers, money saving metrics, and company awards.

---

### Helpful Hint: *Creating Hyperlinks Summary Sheets*

To create Hyperlink Summary Sheets in **Netscape Communicator** you first open a **Netscape Composer** window by selecting the icon noted in figure 2.9. (Please note that you can create Hyperlink Summary Sheets in **Microsoft** as well. Simply, open **WORD**, create the sheet, and then save it as a type HTML document. The concepts in this Helpful Hint apply to both **Netscape** and **Microsoft**.)

> **Figure 2.9: Netscape Communicator's Composer** Icon shown at the bottom of your browser screen.

Figure 2.10 shows the **Composer** window where you will create your sheets. Many of the sites you include should be from your company's website and will include product pages. Recall the section in this chapter on organizing sitemarks. It noted that your sitemark manager can be organized to contain files of pages from your company's website, most notably the products you sell. Your Hyperlinks Summary Sheets should be organized like your sitemark manager. Organize it so you can quickly copy the links and descriptions for pasting into e-mails.

The next step after creating the summary sheets is to put them in a place to which you can easily go when you want to copy and paste. **Composer** is an html publishing board. This means that whatever you create in it is saved as html and can be opened in your browser as a web page. For example, when I went to save figure 2.10 I selected File, Save As..., and named the file. I created a folder named **Hyperlink Summary Sheets** and placed the file in it. The files are saved as browser files (could be **Netscape**, **Explorer**, or any browser you have set as default). Please see figure 2.11 for a look at how these files are represented in **Windows Explorer**.

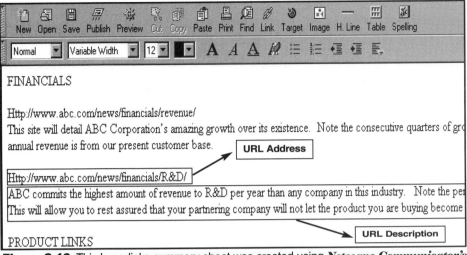

**Figure 2.10:** This hyperlinks summary sheet was created using *Netscape Communicator's Composer.* The content noted above can be copied directly from your browser into an e-mail. Note the website addresses listed as they would be seen in the address bar. When pasted into an e-mail they become hyperlinks.

The next step is to open these files by double clicking them while in **Windows Explorer.** The file will appear as if it was a web page from a site out on the Internet. The address bar will show you from where the file has come (in this case file: ///Dl/Hyperlinks Summary Sheets/Product A.html). Please see figure 2.12 for an example.

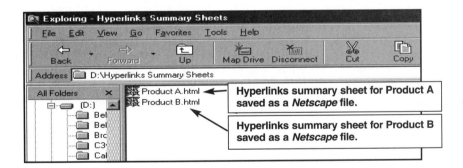

**Figure 2.11:** A look at **Windows Explorer** showing file named **"Hyperlinks Summary Sheets."** Note the files saved as HTML. They are represented as files of your default browser which, in this case, is *Netscape Communicator.*

49

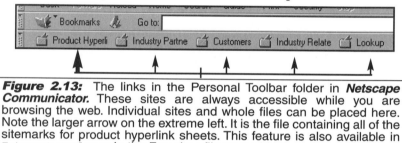

**Figure 2.12:** A look at **Netscape Communicator's** title bar showing a file address. Note that it doesn't contain http://www in front of it. This is because that is only shown when pulling websites down from the World Wide Web for viewing. Http is the protocol used and www represents "World Wide Web." Files from your own computer will note that it is a file and the drive on which it is saved. The file here is saved in "file: ///D|/."

After pulling the file for viewing into your browser you should then sitemark it. In your sitemarks manager you will find a file named Personal Toolbar Folder (for **Netscape**) or Links (for **Internet Explorer**), respectively. These files contain all of the sitemarks shown on your toolbar. Please see figure 2.13 for a toolbar example.

**Figure 2.13:** The links in the Personal Toolbar folder in **Netscape Communicator.** These sites are always accessible while you are browsing the web. Individual sites and whole files can be placed here. Note the larger arrow on the extreme left. It is the file containing all of the sitemarks for product hyperlink sheets. This feature is also available in Internet Explorer in the Favorites file named Links.

Personal Toolbar usage could have its own chapter. However, you get the point if you note, from figures 2.13 and 2.14, the types of sitemarks to keep on it. Product Hyperlinks Sheets, Industry Partners, Customers, Industry Related, and Lookup (search for people, business, etc.) websites are files noted in the example.

Create the files by following the same steps noted in the Helpful Hint titled "Menu Picks to Create Sitemark Files" in **Explorer** and *Netscape Communicator* in this chapter. The only difference is that you are creating these files as a subfolder of your Personal Toolbar folder. Note figure 2.14 to see how the menu views when selecting from the toolbar. The possibilities are endless.

1. Review pages on your website and determine appropriate titles (such as products, press releases, and other) under which they can be categorized.

2. Go back to the browser and look at the address. It may not be the original address such as **http://www.abc.com**. What it may

be is an extension of your company's page. It may read, for example, **http://www.abc.com/tv/listings/.** Copy this address into your *Composer* or **Word** document. Below the link you should write a description.

3. After compiling a few specific sites and descriptions, start filing the sites according to the categories determined in your review.

4. If you have sitemarked sites that you plan to include in a Hyperlink Summary Sheet, you can save time by pasting the sitemark folder from the browser (noted in chapter 2) into the *Composer* or **Word** document and using the pasted hyperlinks.

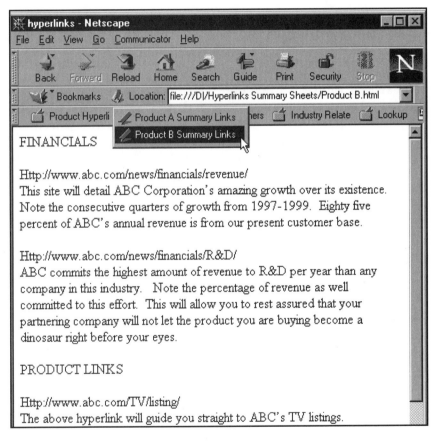

*Figure 2.14:* A file of **Hyperlink Summary Sheet** in the Personal Toolbar folder in *Netscape Communicator.* Note the Product A and Product B Summary links. By placing a file like this on your personal toolbar you ensure easy access to all of your **Hyperlink Summary Sheets.**

### *Sitemarks Saved and Sent*

The value of prospecting from the web has already been established in this book. Another method to enhance prospecting is by creating, via a disk, a 'homemade' website that includes all of the best prospecting websites in your market.

As you search the web you will find websites valuable to your marketing efforts. You'll save these sites and visit them frequently while you prospect. Some are search engines. Others are financial information guides and industry specific websites. The list is endless.

Many network marketers can benefit from gathering websites used by some of their associates and issuing it in universal format to all of their downline distributors. Presently, downlines are expected to find these sites on their own. This is inefficient.

An example of this is when new distributors are signed up. They can benefit from knowing what websites experienced network marketers in the industry utilize. Many downlines spend much of their first year looking through phone books, cold calling without a strategy, and in essence taking pot shots in a prospecting game that sometimes feels like "pin the tail on the donkey." I'll bet you know many people doing it this way today. You may be one of them.

Eliminate this inefficiency by creating a sitemark file to send out to new distributors.

---

## Helpful Hint: *Sending Sitemarks*

Send an e-mail out to all the distributors within your reach and ask them to send you all of their best websites. Categorize the sites you receive and make a page.

The way to have your distributors send you their sitemarked websites is to have them search by doing the following:

1. Go to Find on the **Start** menu in the left hand corner of the desktop.
2. Look for Files and Folders...
3. Input **Bookmark** or **Favorites** (depends on whether you use *Netscape Communicator* or **Explorer** or both).
4. What will be found are all of the files that contain the name

bookmark (*Netscape)* and favorite (**Explorer**). One of those files will be C:\WINDOWS\ and/or *Netscape Communicator's* Bookmarks file in: C:\Program Files\Netscape\Users\default. These files contain all of your sitemarks.

5. Have a floppy disk in the disk drive.

6. Go to the File command and select Send To.

7. Send it to a floppy disk by selecting 3 1/2 Floppy or send it to an e-mail recipient by selecting Mail Recipient.

8. You can then distribute a disk or an e-mail to everyone with the best sites on it.

9. Recipients will open the file from the floppy disk or the e-mail.

See figure 2.15 for an example.

**Note: Companies can make standard sitemark folders of their own website and release them to their independent business owners for their use in hyperlinking to prospects.**

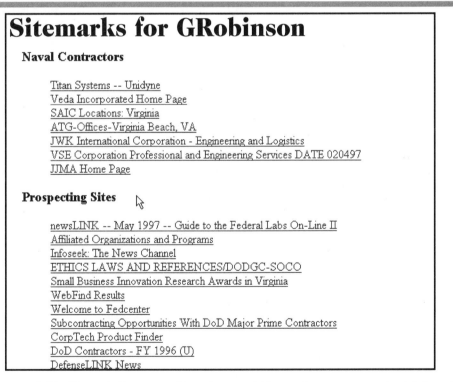

# Sitemarks for GRobinson

**Naval Contractors**

Titan Systems -- Unidyne
Veda Incorporated Home Page
SAIC Locations: Virginia
ATG-Offices-Virginia Beach, VA
JWK International Corporation - Engineering and Logistics
VSE Corporation Professional and Engineering Services DATE 020497
JJMA Home Page

**Prospecting Sites**

newsLINK -- May 1997 -- Guide to the Federal Labs On-Line II
Affiliated Organizations and Programs
Infoseek: The News Channel
ETHICS LAWS AND REFERENCES/DODGC-SOCO
Small Business Innovation Research Awards in Virginia
WebFind Results
Welcome to Fedcenter
Subcontracting Opportunities With DoD Major Prime Contractors
CorpTech Product Finder
DoD Contractors - FY 1996 (U)
DefenseLINK News

*Figure 2.15:* Sitemark files opened in a browser. This can be a very organized listing of sitemarks.

**53**

After creating a prospecting page, you and your distributors can review it on a regular basis. You should frequently update it. It is an incredibly efficient system.

## History Files

Have you ever been searching the web and thought of a site you visited recently that had some information you just had to have? Have you ever spent time looking for that website but you couldn't find it again? If you are like the other 99% of us, you have wasted precious time looking for sites that you had already found. The problem is that you didn't sitemark the address.

## Finding Valuable Sites that You Have Visited but Didn't

## Sitemark When You Were There the First Time

A good browser will keep a running history of the sites you visit. In **Netscape Communicator** you can find these by selecting Communicator on the toolbar and selecting History. A screen appears that includes the sites visited within a pre-determined time period (e.g. 90 days). (**Internet Explorer** has this feature icon above the History file tree.)

Other information is included such as Title, First Visited, Last Visited, Expiration, and Visit Count as you can see in figure 2.16.

**Explorer's** method of recording history is similar to **Netscape Communicator.** One added feature in **Explorer** History is that it organizes the sites into a "Today" file, a last week's file and includes several weeks of file folders.

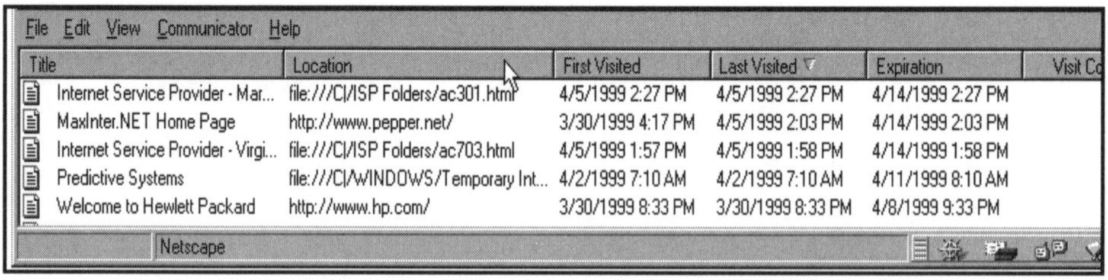

| Title | Location | First Visited | Last Visited ▽ | Expiration | Visit Co |
|-------|----------|---------------|----------------|------------|----------|
| Internet Service Provider - Mar... | file:///C|/ISP Folders/ac301.htm | 4/5/1999 2:27 PM | 4/5/1999 2:27 PM | 4/14/1999 2:27 PM | |
| MaxInter.NET Home Page | http://www.pepper.net/ | 3/30/1999 4:17 PM | 4/5/1999 2:03 PM | 4/14/1999 2:03 PM | |
| Internet Service Provider - Virgi... | file:///C|/ISP Folders/ac703.html | 4/5/1999 1:57 PM | 4/5/1999 1:58 PM | 4/14/1999 1:58 PM | |
| Predictive Systems | file:///C|/WINDOWS/Temporary Int... | 4/2/1999 7:10 AM | 4/2/1999 7:10 AM | 4/11/1999 8:10 AM | |
| Welcome to Hewlett Packard | http://www.hp.com/ | 3/30/1999 8:33 PM | 3/30/1999 8:33 PM | 4/8/1999 9:33 PM | |

File  Edit  View  Communicator  Help

Netscape

*Figure 2.16: **Netscape Communicator** History Window.*

## **Helpful Hint:** *History Search*

You can combine any number of choices (please see figure 2.17) to determine search criteria for a selected word. By selecting the **more** or **fewer** icons you can link multiple selection criteria to determine the sites for which you are looking. Figure 2.18 provides an example.

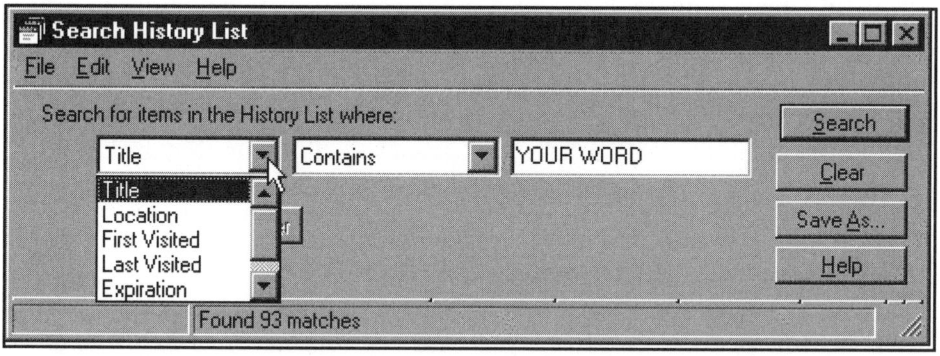

**Figure 2.17:** *Netscape Communicator* History Search Menu.

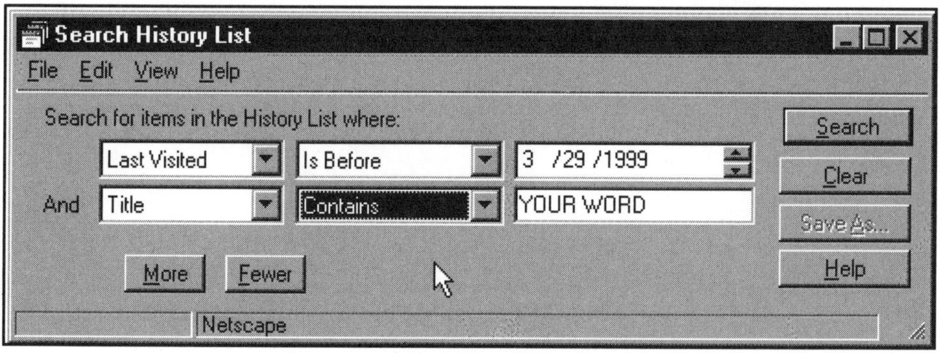

**Figure 2.18:** *Netscape Communicator* History Search Menu with multiple selection criteria.

**55**

## Summary

Chapter two builds on techniques introduced in chapter one.

It starts with copying and pasting from programs. Among the important things to copy and paste are website addresses, e-mail addresses, pictures, and material from websites. Multiple how-to helpful hints are noted. By knowing how to copy and paste, the network marketer starts to become more effective and more efficient.

Sitemarking pointers such as how to create sitemarks, naming files, organizing files, what to mark, and using sitemarks are explained. The important point is to use sitemarks in e-mail. By copying sitemark files into e-mail, the network marketer creates many hyperlinks in one step. This is a replacement for manual processes such as mailing and faxing.

Hyperlink Summary Sheets takes this concept one step further. This tactic is for the network marketer who likes to send detailed descriptions with hyperlinks.

The next subject covered is a website history file. A search function exists within browsers so that you can retrieve websites you want to revisit but don't remember the address. This allows you to find the site and mark it.

The network marketer, after reading chapters 1 & 2, knows how to utilize the tactics that will eliminate the need for mailing marketing material. This will save them much money and even more time.

# 3

# Mission: Re'Search' and Enjoy.

"People who work sitting down get paid more than people who work standing up."
   Ogden Nash

"All the best work is done the way the ants do things-by tiny but untiring and regular additions."
   Lafcadio Hearn

"My father taught me to work, he didn't teach me to love it."
   Abraham Lincoln

"It was on the Internet."
   Bill Robinson, (Vice President and Controller)

How smart would you be if you had more information available to you than the Libraries of Congress, Harvard, and Yale? Would researching prospects be easier? I estimate that those three libraries need millions of dollars a year to support them.

What if you could get this information for free? To top that, what if you could fit all of it into a laptop computer on your desk? All you need is a computer and a phone line to tap into an information source larger than these libraries. That information source is the Internet.

Chapters one and two concentrated on how you can provide information to your contacts more easily and efficiently. This chapter will focus on how to gather important information for prospecting.

## *Search Engines*

Search engines provide a wealth of research information for the network marketer. You will have a choice. Here are some of them:

| | |
|---|---|
| Yahoo | http://www.yahoo.com |
| Infoseek | http://www.infoseek.com |
| Altavista | http://www.altavista.com/ |
| Lycos | http://www.lycos.com |
| Excite | http://www.excite.com |
| Euroseek | http://www.euroseek.net/page?ifl=uk |
| Mining Co. | http://miningco.com/ |
| WorldPages | http://www.worldpages.com |
| NetGuide | http://www.netguide.com |
| Yack | http://www.yack.com |
| Northern Light | http://www.northernlight.com |
| Encarta | http://www.encarta.com/ |
| LookSmart | http://www.looksmart.com/ |
| Web Events | http://webevents.msn.com/ |
| Ask Jeeves | http://www.ask.com |

When queried, each of these search engines will provide some different sites than the others. You may come to like one best based on the information typically requested.

# Helpful Hint: *Narrow Your Search*

The web is a world wide tool. For example, when you search via a common word, such as CANON, the search will return any sites that include that word, no matter how relevant the page is to CANON Inc. To avoid this you must narrow your search by including more exclusive words. Using Canon as an example, a person might include "INC." e.g. "CANON INC." (see figure 3.1). You will have to put both words in quotations and it will then return much more specific websites.

**Figure 3.1:** Example of how to narrow the search for Canon.

A good example of how this hint helps is:
- When searching in **Infoseek** for CANON, without other specific words, 274,413 web pages were returned.
- When including INC. and quotation marks 1,049 web pages were returned.

This is much more efficient and will be a great time saver when searching. So when querying a search engine, you should narrow the search early.

After receiving a list of sites from a query, you should begin to review the links. Keep in mind that the higher the link, the more likely it is related to the subject you queried. Figure 3.2 is an example.

Companies and individuals register their websites with search engines by prioritizing words that relate to their sites. For example, if Canon was registering their site with **Yahoo!**, they might provide a list of words. The idea is to provide words people would typically use to find a site like Canon. A sample of the words they might provide is:

1. Canon
2. Printers

3. Pictures

4. Film

5. Hewlett Packard (Good idea here. If someone were querying HP, Canon's website would appear also).

6. Computers

**Web search results**    1 - 10 of **857** results most relevant to **"canon inc."**
Next 10 >  |  Hide summaries  |  Sort by date  |  Ungroup results

**Canon U.S.A., Inc.**
Cameras, office equipment, technology equipment and more.
100% **Date: 11 Jan 1999**, Size 0.8K, http://www.usa.canon.com/        1st ranked
Find similar pages  |  Grouped results from www.usa.canon.com

**Welcome to Canon NEXTSTEP Developer Support**
at Kanagawa Japan. We are so happy to help you with the Japanese Version of NEXTSTEP. NEX
Maintained by MM Group **Canon.Inc**
96% **Date: 1 Oct 1997**, Size 2.6K, http://www.cnds.canon.co.jp/        2nd ranked
Find similar pages

**----------» Corporate profiles Annual Report 1997 Information from our business ...**
**Canon Inc's** homepage You can find information of **Canon** group from all over the world. ex)produ
96% **Date: 5 Feb 1999**, Size 14.0K, http://www.canon.co.jp/index-e.html
Find similar pages  |  Grouped results from www.canon.co.jp

**CANON INC Research Data**
**CANON INC** demographics, profiles, business data, advertising and mailing lists are available abo
76% **Date: 30 Dec 1998**, Size 34.3K, http://www.usadata.com/usadata2000/advertiser/canonin

***Figure 3.2:*** Example of how search engines prioritize relevant messages. The higher they are in the query, the more relevant they are to your word.

Canon would hope that whenever you type in one of their words that their site would appear high on the query, thus improving the chance of you browsing their site.

### Information on the Web

All of the information you want to know about is on the web. Search engines and financial pages are especially helpful. An example is **Yahoo! Finance.** It provides a section for publicly traded companies. Information included is:

• Company Profile: A brief description of the company.

• Company News: The most recent press releases.

• Stock Price: Scroll down to **Company Info** and input a company.

The first step is to input the company name and obtain the company ticker symbol (see figure 3.3).

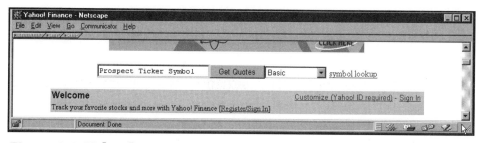

***Figure 3.3: Yahoo!*** window for discovering a company's public trading symbol.

Once you input the ticker and select Get Quotes, the query will return the company's stock price. (see figure 3.4)

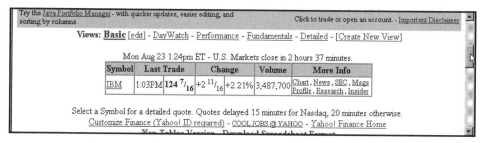

***Figure 3.4: Yahoo! Finance*** stock price window. **More Info** provides great tools for researching.

Other information is available. **More Info** provides a rich source of prospect information. Included is: <u>Chart</u> (View graphs on the stock performance over designated time periods); <u>News</u> (company press releases); <u>SEC</u> (prospect quarterly reports to the SEC); <u>Msgs</u> (**Yahoo!** visitor message board); <u>Profile</u> (contains the most information for the network marketer who sells to businesses; we'll revisit this in a moment); <u>Research</u> (corporate performance summary); and <u>Insider</u> (company top officer trading register). All of the links have information about the prospect.

61

As mentioned before, the <u>Profile</u> section is the most valuable. Figure 3.5 provides a look at what is included.

```
┌─────────────────────────────────────────────────────────────────────────┐
│ IBM                                                              NYSE : IBM│
├─────────────────────────────────────────────────────────────────────────┤
│                                                                           │
│      Address: One New Orchard Road          Financial Links               │
│               Armonk, NY 10504              · Company News                │
│        Phone: (914) 499-1900                · Research Report             │
│          Fax: (914) 765-6021                · Upgrade/Downgrade History   │
│       Sector: Technology                    · Latest Stock Price          │
│     Industry: Computer Hardware             · Insider Trades              │
│    Employees: 291,067                       · SEC Filings (raw filings)   │
│     Officers: Louis V. Gerstner Jr., Chmn./CEO  · Corporate Financials    │
│               Lawrence R. Ricciardi,        · Message Board               │
│               Sr. VP/CFO/Counsel                                          │
│               John E. Hickey, VP/Secy.      Company's Web Presence        │
│               Jeffrey D. Serkes, VP/Treas.  · Home Page                   │
│               Mark Loughridge, VP/Contr.    · Investor Relations          │
│                                             · Employment                  │
│                                             · Products & Services         │
│                                             · Subsidiaries                │
│                                             · Divisions                   │
│                                                                           │
│                                             · Yahoo! Category             │
│                                             · Search Yahoo! for related links...│
│                                                                           │
└─────────────────────────────────────────────────────────────────────────┘
```

*Figure 3.5:* A **Yahoo!** Finance company profile. This is a very valuable information gathering tool for companies of interest.

<u>Sector</u> notes the company's sector and lists the industries within that sector. Query industries that are likely prospects and you will be provided with a list of public companies. You can review every company and find the same information noted above. This will help when prospecting.

<u>Industry</u> section is the category the company is in the sector.

<u>Company News</u>, <u>Research Report</u>, <u>Upgrade/Downgrade History</u>, <u>Latest Stock Price</u>, <u>Insider Trades</u>, <u>SEC Filings</u>, <u>Corporate Financials</u>, and <u>Message Board</u> are links back to the information provided on the main page.

**Company's Web Presence** is an extremely helpful section. First, the company's <u>Home Page</u> is provided, which isn't always easy to find. <u>Investor Relations</u> is the official investor relations link. <u>Product & Services</u> breaks down products by category. <u>Subsidiaries</u> lists all of its companies. This is especially powerful for network marketers whose companies have corporate pricing agreements. <u>Divisions</u> lists the divisions within the company you are researching. This helps you quickly narrow your search to the divisions where your product best applies.

The final two categories are **Yahoo!** Category and Search **Yahoo!** for related links.... These two links take you to the **Yahoo!** category search page and then provide you with related links. Related links include industry-related websites, competitors, and others. This is a goldmine for the network marketer.

## Companies at a Glance

All successful network marketers have looked forward to the day when they needed to track their large portfolio and are looking for quicker ways to do so. **Yahoo!** provides an easy way to view all of your stock's performance on a regular basis. The steps are as follows:

1. Go to the **Yahoo! Finance** page
2. Select Customize in the top right hand corner.
3. Obtain a **Yahoo!** account name and login at **Yahoo!** Account Information.
4. Once you obtain your account go to Portfolio in the Customize section.
5. Select Create New Portfolio.
6. You can categorize your portfolios according to sector invested or by companies of interest. The network marketer that sells to public companies can also categorize according to prospect and customer. For example, you can create a customers and prospects portfolio. Other good ideas would be to create a competitors portfolio, customer or prospect competitors portfolio, or industry sector portfolios. The possibilities are endless.

See figure 3.6 for an example.

| Symbol | Last Trade | | Change | | Volume | More Info |
|--------|------------|---|--------|---|--------|-----------|
| SUNW | May 21 | 60 $^3/_{16}$ | -1 $^3/_4$ | -2.83% | 6,454,600 | Chart, News, SEC, Msgs Profile, Research, Insider |
| DELL | May 21 | 37 $^5/_{16}$ | $-^{15}/_{16}$ | -2.45% | 37,864,800 | Chart, News, SEC, Msgs Profile, Research, Insider |
| CPQ | May 21 | 25 $^1/_{16}$ | $-^7/_{16}$ | -1.72% | 7,803,700 | Chart, News, SEC, Msgs Profile, Research, Insider |
| SGI | May 21 | 11 $^{13}/_{16}$ | $-^3/_{16}$ | -1.56% | 356,500 | Chart, News, SEC, Msgs Profile, Research, Insider |
| NOVL | May 21 | 24 $^5/_8$ | $-^1/_8$ | -0.51% | 2,318,000 | Chart, News, SEC, Msgs Profile, Research, Insider |
| MSFT | May 21 | 77 $^9/_{16}$ | $-^7/_8$ | -1.12% | 28,284,800 | Chart, News, SEC, Msgs Profile, Research, Insider |
| CSCO | May 21 | 113 $^1/_4$ | -1 $^1/_2$ | -1.31% | 11,452,200 | Chart, News, SEC, Msgs Profile, Research, Insider |
| LU | May 21 | 57 $^9/_{16}$ | -1 $^7/_{16}$ | -2.44% | 7,640,300 | Chart, News, SEC, Msgs Profile, Research, Insider |
| NEON | May 21 | 39 $^1/_4$ | -3 $^5/_8$ | -8.45% | 1,298,500 | Chart, News, SEC, Msgs Profile, Research, Insider |
| PMTC | May 21 | 13 $^3/_{16}$ | $-^{17}/_{32}$ | -3.87% | 4,649,200 | Chart, News, SEC, Msgs Profile, Research, Insider |

**Figure 3.6:** A **Yahoo!** Finance stock price portfolio makes for easy viewing of companies' stock prices in your portfolio.

## Summary

The web contains an amazing amount of information that can help you succeed. Search engines are the way to tap into this information. This chapter focuses on the best searching methods.

First, there are many search engines out on the web that can help you find valuable information. This chapter lists a few of the better known sites.

Querying those search engines can produce over 200,000 websites. It is best to narrow a search early. You can narrow your search by including related words and putting quotation marks around the phrase.

There are methods on how search engines prioritize sites for your query. These are based on trigger words supplied by the registering company.

Finally, **Yahoo! Finance** provides a wealth of information on publicly traded companies. Included are profiles, financial performance, websites, and subsidiaries. This program can be customized to view daily your hottest stocks performance.

Information and research is the weapon against competition to better strategize, present, and eventually close more business. Knowing how to utilize search engines will help you obtain this information.

# 4

# Prospecting:
# The New Fashioned Way.

*"A study of the map will indicate where critical situations exist or are apt to develop, and so indicate where the commander should be."*
*General George S. Patton, Jr.: War As I Knew It, 1947*

*"The amount of intelligence necessary to please us is a most accurate measure of the amount of intelligence we have ourselves."*
*Helvetius*

*"Time spent on reconnaissance is seldom wasted."*
*British Army Field Service Regulations, 1912*

*"You can never do too much reconnaissance."*
*General George S. Patton, Jr.: War As I Knew It, 1947*

There is nobody better than one of the most famous generals in United States history to speak of the importance of preparation, research and strategy. Like Patton, the network marketer is a commander. He is a commander of the process and needs to treat it like a campaign.

The relationship marketing campaign, like a military campaign, requires tactical planning maneuvers. The difference is in the intelligence tools used.

I came across some tools listed in this chapter when, in one of my jobs, Lockheed Martin was a major prospect for my product. I knew that if I blanketed my area for Lockheed I could ensure that I wouldn't miss an opportunity. I would go to the library and manually research Lockheed's locations. I would spend hours on weekends determining where the Lockheed Martin locations were in the state. This exercise was time consuming until I stumbled upon the Internet phone book. What I found was that I could perform a couple hours of library research in fifteen minutes using the Internet. I instantly realized a 90% reduction in time spent prospecting while getting the same results.

After this revelation I religiously used the Internet in the prospecting process.

### Internet Phone Books

The Internet contains many phone book sites. These phone books serve as listings similar to the Yellow Pages. Internet phone book sites search for businesses by territory. They give you access to excellent information on prospects in your area. The sites can do the following:

• Query territories via a prospect category.

• Give name, address, and directions for all results in the query.

Sitemark the following site: http://yp.uswest.com/cgi/searcg.fcg (see figure 4.1).

Tools like this allow you to look for prospects by **Search by Category** or **Search by Name** functions.

**Searching by Category** is the process of querying via an industry type. For example, if you sold life insurance to small businesses and you managed to make a specialty out of delicatessens with under 30 employees you could input "delicatessens" for the category requested. You would then input city and state (Trenton, NJ in this example). Some tools provide sub-category options, thus another level of qualification by choosing sub-categories that contain better prospects. (See figure 4.2)

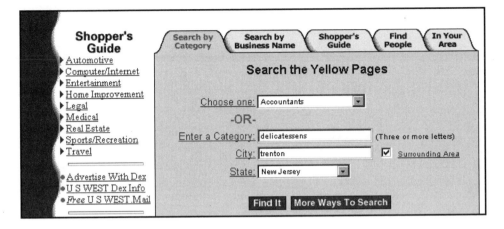

**Figure 4.1:** Internet phone books are an excellent tool to query in towns where you are marketing.

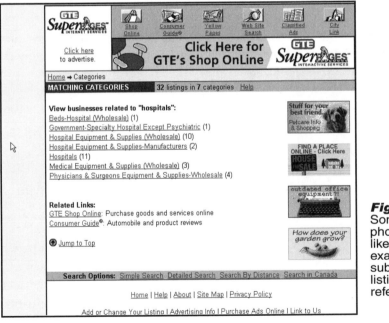

**Figure 4.2:** Some Internet phone books, like in this example, will sub-categorize listings for easier reference.

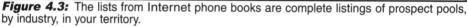

**Figure 4.3:** The lists from Internet phone books are complete listings of prospect pools, by industry, in your territory.

Online phone books can provide a complete list of company locations in a specified area. This is a very effective way to obtain prospect lists with addresses, phone numbers, and directions.

Figure 4.3 is an example of the information received from the delicatessen query in Trenton, NJ.

Along with the address and phone number you will find <u>See Map</u>. The map includes an overview of the location area with surrounding streets and the position of the building on that street (see figure 4.4).

At the top right hand corner of this page you find the link named <u>Driving Directions</u>.

When selecting this link you see a screen, which automatically places the destination address. The other information needed is a starting address and your choice of Door-to-Door or City-to-City directions.

Once the directions query is finished you will be provided with a complete map of the destination area of where you are going. In addition, you can query to see a larger or a smaller view of the area based on preference.

You can also request a detailed directions report complete with turn by turn directions and mileage, similar to what is shown in figures 4.4 and 4.5.

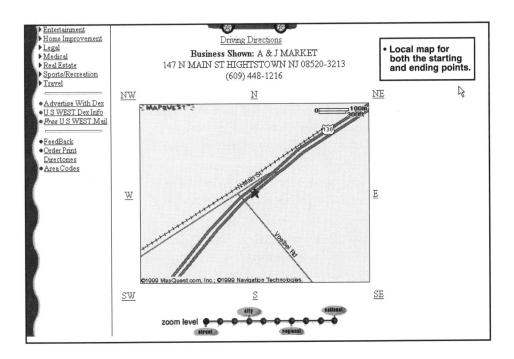

**Figure 4.5** (above) and **4.5** (below): The bullets noted in these pictures describe the direction information provided.

Suggestions on where this is helpful is for you to copy and paste the directions from airports or other call locations to customer sites into an e-mail and send it to associates which may be joining you on a call. It is a professional gesture that is impressive and takes little time. Some map sites even allow you to forward the page as a hyperlink (check this first, as some map sites don't allow this).

## Finding People

Accessing contact information for people is easy using web tools. The Internet has many sites that enable you to query for a person's phone number, address, or e-mail address. Just about every search engine contains this capability.

Simply select the link to the query engine. Enter as much information as you have for the person you are trying to find. Then select **Find**. It is that easy.

Don't get frustrated if your first few searches don't yield the information for which you are looking. It is important to recognize that some search engines are more up-to-date than others. It is wise to keep many search engines sitemarked. Try multiple engines for your query. Chances are you will find the information for which you are searching.

Please also note that an e-mail address is often the most difficult information to gather from these tools. With the amount of customer churn Internet service providers have been having it has been hard for *people search engines* to keep up-to-date databases. It is obvious that when customers change providers their e-mail addresses change also. So, as a result, it is often times hard to reference people's e-mail addresses.

---

### Helpful Hint: *Source Sites*

**Directions:**
*Map Quest* This is the most commonly used directions web site.

Gives estimated time based on average MPH.

> http://www.mapquest.com/

***City Guide***  This is an excellent site with up-to-date directions. Gives estimated time based on average MPH.

> http://cg.zip2.com/whowhere/scripts/staticpage.dll?ep=8200&ck=17
> 357549&userid=30207140&userpw=xtv0J_txAwt8tE_FD0C&versio
> n=606022&adrVer=901014779&ver=cg0.1

The City Guide site is a long URL address, but all you have to do is type it into your address bar once, travel to the address, and sitemark the site. When you sitemark it save it in the Personal Toolbar Folder and it will always be on the screen as a link you can visit.

| | |
|---|---|
| ***Mapblast*** | http://www.mapblast.com |
| ***DeLorme*** | http://www.delorme.com |
| ***Yahoo! Maps*** | http://maps.yahoo.com |
| ***Mapsonus*** | http://www.mapsonus.com/ |

## Finding People:

| | |
|---|---|
| ***Bigfoot*** | http://search.bigfoot.com/SEARCH |

<u>All-Purpose sites</u> including Find a Business, Finding People's E-mail addresses and contact information, Directions and Maps, Yellow Pages:

| | |
|---|---|
| ***GTE Superpages*** | http://superpages.gte.net/ |
| *US WEST* | http://yp.uswest.com/cgi/search.fcg |

## Travel:

| | |
|---|---|
| ***Amtrak*** | http://www.amtrak.com/ |
| ***Fodors Travel Online*** | http://www.fodors.com |
| ***Leisure Plan*** | http://www.leisureplan.com |
| ***Travel Reservations*** | http://www.reservations.com/ |
| ***Travelocity*** | http://www.travelocity.com/ |
| ***The Weather Channel*** | http://www.weather.com/twc/ homepage.twc |

## Miscellaneous:

| | |
|---|---|
| ***Federal Express*** | http://www.fedex.com |
| ***Library of Congress*** | http://lcweb.loc.gov/homepage/ lchp.html |
| ***Money Online*** | http://www.money.com |

*USPS*                    http://www.usps.gov/

## Pre-Planning Your Week

Pre-planning with the aforementioned tools can make life much easier for the network marketer. Note the information available from the above sites:

- Prospect related information such as names, location, and phone number.
- Detailed maps and directions to customer locations which include:
  - Turn by turn instructions.
  - Approximate travel time.
  - Overview maps.

The following is the **Virtual Pre-Planning Check list.** The steps are as follows:

1. List **Geographic areas** to market in this week:

   **M:** Trenton, NJ, **T:** Camden, NJ, **W:** Philadelphia, PA, **R:** Princeton, NJ, **F:** Dover, NJ

2. **Appointments** for the week:
   - Determine amount of time you will need for each appointment.
   - Determine other areas near the appointment locations that have prospects to which you want to market.

3. Go to **http://yp.uswest.com/cgi/search.fcg**, which is a **phone book** on the web. Select the business search or people search depending on your intention.
   - (If you don't market to businesses please go to step 9).

4. **Industry types** to market to during the week.
   - If you sell to multiple industry types, categorize them. e.g. Banks, Hospitals, Manufacturing, etc.
   - Note the products that have been your hot sellers recently.
   - Scan **hot markets** lists supplied by your company's marketing department.

5. **Input the cities into the phone book:**

   | Trenton                    I |

   **Enter City** (Optional)

6. **Input categories** from your industry types list (if you sell to businesses):

Enter Category (Top Categories)

7. **Query the phone book** to produce your prospect lists.

8. **Choose prospects** from the lists.

   • Go to step 10.

9. **Input people** from the list of appointments you have (if you sell to homes).

10. Get directions from **City Guide, Map Quest,** or a directions search engine of your choice.

   • If you don't know where the prospect is located, get directions by inputting your starting address, i.e. prospect, airport, office and then the address of your next call. Do this for all of your weekly calls. This is especially useful if you are marketing out of town.

   • Use Copy and Paste functions to copy addresses from generated lists to **City Guide** or **Map Quest**. This will save time versus manually typing the addresses. Hint: Use the Back and Forward buttons on your browser to jump from the provided list to the City Guide.

When you utilize this pre-planning technique, you will be able to pre-plan much more quickly than in the past. You will reduce the unpredictable delays of getting lost when traveling to a call. You will get more prospect face time and are assured of blanketing your territory.

### Summary

Internet tools provide a wealth of information for the network marketer. Using the Internet phone book, network marketers begin to realize how much information is at their fingertips. These phone books aid in blanketing a territory via industry type or by company name. If you market to residences the phone books aid you when gathering complete information about your prospect. Lists provide addresses, phone numbers, directions, and locations for people and for businesses. They can be specific based on the location queried, such as state or city. Many people finder sites now allow you to add the contact information directly to your contact manager, such as **Outlook**.

Pre-planning is an excellent exercise to aid in time management. The Internet offers many tools that, if used together, can help the network marketer pre-plan their weeks.

Tools like online maps, travel planning sites, and people finder will save you travel time and increase face to face time with your prospects.

# Unique uses of *Excel* with a little bit of *Word* as Network Marketing Tools

*"You will always do much, if you accomplish perfectly what you do."*
  A.D. Sertillanges

*"When a thing is thoroughly well done it often has the air of being a miracle."*
  Arnold Bennett

*"Hit the ball over the fence and you can take your time running the bases."*
  John W. Raper

*"Opportunities are usually disguised as hard work, so most people don't recognize them."*
  Ann Landers

As a new sales person, I was faced with the challenge of mastering time management. Organizational skills were crucial to my success and it was quickly evident it was my weakest area. I would visit Staples and Office Max and buy gadgets that I thought would solve my problems. Included in the long list of purchases were day timers, filing cabinets, and many other expensive items. Nothing seemed to solve the problem. The lack of organization was affecting my performance and it culminated in one three month period when I didn't make any sales.

It wasn't long after this that I acquired a computer. In the three months following, I incorporated many of the tactics you will find in this chapter. The sales that resulted were incredible. Not only did I sell my way into keeping a job, but I also broke records in the process. The final quarter of that year I was able to sell, in three consecutive months, three of my division's biggest deals. I made leaders list in three product categories.

This was proof enough to me that the computer was not only an advantage in the selling process, but a necessity.

### **Excel** in Network Marketing

**Excel** programs are computer generated spreadsheets. They can be the hardest tool from **Microsoft Office** for the network marketer to master. Use them correctly and it will help propel you to a higher level. This next section suggests ideas on how to use this tool.

### Use Spreadsheets To Be More Efficient

Network Marketers know that organization is a key to success. The information that needs to be tracked consumes time and can be an inhibitor if not managed correctly. Until the advent of the personal computer, network marketers tracked information using paper and files. **Excel** makes those methods outdated.

Spreadsheets are the backbone of **Excel**. They are defined as programs that organize numbers, labels, and formulas in rows and columns for calculating results. They are very suitable for the home business person and especially the network marketer.

As I reviewed many of the information tracking methods available to the network marketer, some rose above the others. The following is a group of lists that are common for network marketers to track:

- Daily Contacts including time logs for direct retail sales.
- Monthly summary of people contacted, time spent, and money earned in making direct retail sales.
- Daily Contacts and time logs for building organizations.
- Monthly summary of persons contacted and time spent in building an organization.

**Excel** is a great tool for managing these lists. The most common format is a Contact & Time Log.

Contact and Time Logs help network marketers to track the time it takes to accomplish certain steps in their marketing cycle. The steps are related to selling their product and signing distributors. These include: people contacted about selling, presentations to interested people, training new distributors, number of sign-ups becoming active distributors, new prospects contacted about products, sales presentations, meeting arrangements, presentations to prospects and number of purchases and total sales.

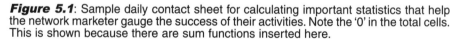

| Contact Sheet and Time Log for Building a Distributor Organization | | | | | | | |
|---|---|---|---|---|---|---|---|
| Month: _____  Week #: _____   Date: _____ | | | | | | | |
| | New People Contacted About Selling | | Presentations to interested people | | New Distributors to be Trained | | Number of New Active Distributors |
| Day of Week | Total People | Level of Effort | Total People | Level of Effort | Total People | Level of Effort | |
| Monday | | | | | | | |
| Tuesday | | | | | | | |
| Wednesday | | | | | | | |
| Thursday | | | | | | | |
| Friday | | | | | | | |
| Saturday | | | | | | | |
| Sunday | | | | | | | |
| Total | 0 | 0 | 0 | 0 | 0 | 0 | 0 |

***Figure 5.1***: Sample daily contact sheet for calculating important statistics that help the network marketer gauge the success of their activities. Note the '0' in the total cells. This is shown because there are sum functions inserted here.

These contact sheets and time logs can be organized in two ways: for sales contacts and for distributor contacts. Figure 5.1 illustrates a distributor oriented contact log.

By using **Excel** you can automatically calculate these totals. Formulas can be programmed into cells. For example, in figure 5.1 you will note zeroes in the **Total** cells on the spreadsheet. The reason they show zero is because there are formulas inserted that add up the cells above it ( **=SUM(Xcell:Ycell)** ) and there is nothing in those cells to add. Note in figure 5.2 what happens when numbers are inserted into the cells above the **Total** cell. The sum of the cells is automatically computed in real time.

The formulas can be copied and pasted to cells where similar formulas will be inserted. For example, if cell C23 contains (=SUM(C16:C22)) and you were to copy it to cell D23 the formula would change to (=SUM(D16:D22)). You can paste to multiple cells simultaneously and the same logic would be applied.

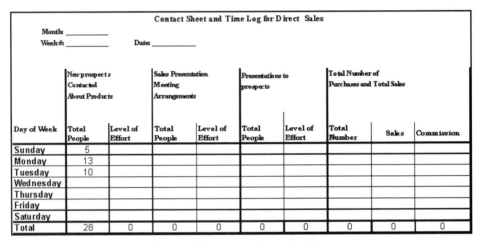

**Figure 5.2:** Sample Daily Contact Sheet showing calculations.

When you create monthly summaries of the daily contact sheets and time logs you can link them to the sheets and logs that apply so that the totals will automatically insert themselves into the summaries.

For example, in figure 5.3 note that the total from figure 5.2 is in the week one **Total** column. A formula (=cell e.g.( =A4)) made that an automatic function. You can create formulas in all of the cells in the monthly summary. This will automate the entire summary.

Once you finish the sheet containing the automated weekly logs and monthly summary you can keep it as a master version in your file. Copy and paste the sheet to twelve other sheets in the **Excel** file. Rename the sheets by double right clicking on the sheet tab in the lower left-hand corner of the window. Name a sheet for each month of the year. Include the year in the name. (See figure 5.5)

| Week | New prospects Contacted About Products | | Presentations to prospects | | Sales Presentation Meeting Arrangements | | Total Number of Purchases and Total Sales | | |
|---|---|---|---|---|---|---|---|---|---|
| | Total People | Level of Effort | Total People | Level of Effort | Total People | Level of Effort | Total Number | Sales | Commission |
| Week 1 | 28 | | | | | | | | |
| Week 2 | | | | | | | | | |
| Week 3 | | | | | | | | | |
| Week 4 | | | | | | | | | |
| Week 5 | | | | | | | | | |
| Total | 28 | 0 | 0 | 0 | 0 | 0 | 0 | 0 | 0 |

**Figure 5.3:** A monthly summary sheet noting a total from one table being copied to another.

NOTE: *Sheets* in **Excel** are the equivalent of *pages* in Word. See figure 5.4.

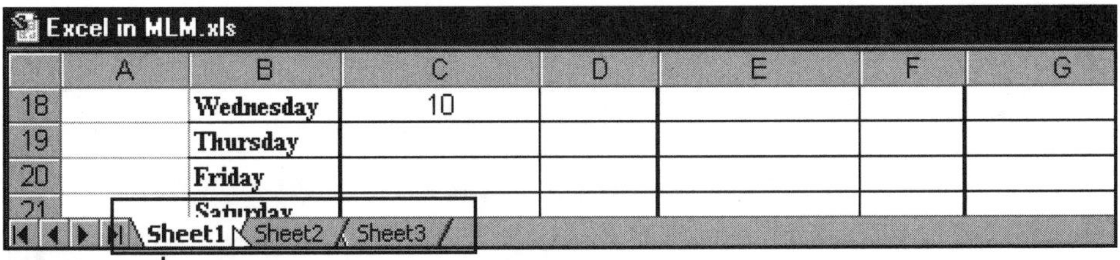

**Figure 5.4:** An **Excel** spreadsheet showing the sheet tabs in the lower left-hand corner. These represent different pages in the spreadsheet.

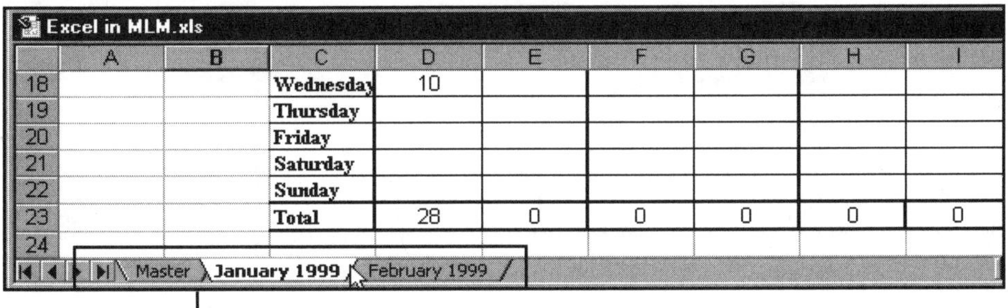

**Figure 5.5:** An **Excel** spreadsheet showing renamed sheet tabs in the lower left-hand corner. Here you can see the master and the first two months of the year.

79

**Contact Sheet and Time Log for Building a Distributor Organization**

Month: _____
Week #: _____        Date: _____

| Day of Week | New People Contacted About Selling | | Presentations to interested people | | New Distributors to be Trained | | Number of New Active Distributors |
|---|---|---|---|---|---|---|---|
| | Total People | Level of Effort | Total People | Level of Effort | Total People | Level of Effort | |
| Monday | | | | | | | |
| Tuesday | | | | | | | |
| Wednesday | | | | | | | |
| Thursday | | | | | | | |
| Friday | | | | | | | |
| Saturday | | | | | | | |
| Sunday | | | | | | | |
| Total | 0 | 0 | 0 | 0 | 0 | 0 | 0 |

**Figure 5.6:** A contact sheet and time log for building a distributor organization.

**Monthly Summary of Contact Sheets and Time Spent for Building A Distributor Organization**

Month: _____
Date: _____

| Week | New prospects Contacted About Products | | Presentations to prospects | | Sales Presentation Meeting Arrangements | |
|---|---|---|---|---|---|---|
| | Total People | Level of Effort | Total People | Level of Effort | Total People | Level of Effort |
| Week 1 | 28 | | | | | |
| Week 2 | | | | | | |
| Week 3 | | | | | | |
| Week 4 | | | | | | |
| Week 5 | | | | | | |
| Total | O | O | O | O | O | O |

**Figure 5.7:** A monthly summary for building a distributor organization.

**Helpful Hint:** *Inserting Addition, Subtraction,*
*Multiplication and Division*

To insert functions into **Excel** spreadsheets:

1. Go to the cell in which you want to insert the function.

2. Type = and then the cell number that is first in the equation.

3. Type +, -- , *, or / (addition, subtraction, multiplication, and division) respectively.

4. Type the next cell in the equation.

5. Hit the Enter key on your keyboard.

Specific functions can be pasted by selecting the function icon. Figure 5.8 shows the icon on the toolbar.

*Figure 5.8:* An **Excel** spreadsheet toolbar showing the function key. This key takes the user to a menu driven formula creation window. It is an excellent tool for the beginner.

## ROI's (Return on Investment) and Justifications

Providing the customer with an easy road to buy your product is crucial in network marketing. I learned the importance of this in the job I mentioned in the beginning of this chapter.

One weekend, during my sales slump, I created an automatic ROI program in **Excel** and on that Monday sent a justification to each prospect that had a proposal from my company. The next quarter I was 200% of quota. Many of the sales were because I gave them justifications.

Many sales cycles progress slowly because prospects don't realize the cost savings a product offers. Even worse, they may know the savings, but don't know how to present it to management for approval. A justification sent with every quotation reduces the likelihood of slow progress. This may not be practical in every industry and with every product, but in many cases a simple ROI will be influential. It also can

81

be used as a template for your prospects to model their own.

Network marketers who typically don't have templates provided by their company can also use these.

How do you generate ROI's quickly?

The automatic ROI is a spreadsheet that can generate justifications quickly by inputting relevant data.   The idea is to create standard formulas that will compute the ROI. Many companies distribute an ROI template to the field, but if your company does not it is wise to create one. **Excel** is ideal for ROI's because cells in **Excel** retain formulas that can be reused.  (Go to any book store and look for a book titled **How to Use Excel** published by Que Company.  This book is an excellent guide to using **Excel**.)

The following questions will help you when you create justifications:

- Where does your product excel versus competitors?

- Where is the major payoff  (timesavings, cost savings, etc.) in your product?

- What is the best way to justify this product to most customers?

- Where could you automate calculations?

- Do median standards exist that, if used, would be effective in a presentation? (e.g. The Chevrolet gets 45 mpg and a Jeep gets 20 mpg).

After creating an ROI, save different versions as templates. When saving, record it as an .xlt file (see figure 5.9). Saving spreadsheets as templates creates automatic ROI's that can be used repeatedly.   Figure 5.10 is an example.

**Figure 5.9:** The save window in **Excel**. Note the highlighted area "Save as Type." You will note that Template is an option. It is saved as an .xlt file (**Excel** template).

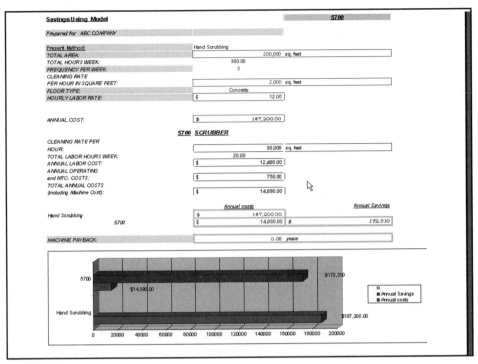

**Figure 5.10:** Sample ROI made in **Microsoft Excel.** In this example, only seven cells needed input to create this ROI. They include product, company name, present method, total area, frequency, floor type and hourly labor rate. Lookup commands helped automate the spreadsheet.

## More *Excel* Time Saving Tricks

If you have a series of cells, such as H4 to H15, to which you would like to apply a formula you don't have to type every cell number. Simply type in the starting cell, colon, and the ending cell. (e.g. H4:H15)

## Competitive Placement Summary Spreadsheets

A key to any marketing effort is the ability to record prospects that buy competitive products (see figure 5.11). **Excel** provides a great way to create these lists. This list can be referenced when:

- Your company releases a new product and you want to reference competitive placements that it could replace.
- Time Limited Offers targeted at a specific competitor.
- Competitor performance in your territory.
- Statistics for your reference.

83

| | A | B | C | D | E |
|---|---|---|---|---|---|
| 1 | | | | | |
| 2 | | **Internet Service Providers** | | | |
| 3 | | | | | |
| 4 | **Company Name** | **Site** | **Area Code** | **Phone** | **Competitor** |
| 5 | | | | | |
| 6 | Verio | http://www.clark.net | 410 | 995-0550 | ABC Networks |
| 7 | CT Technology | http://www.ct-group.com/ | 410 | 568-1800 | 123 Network |
| 8 | Delmarva Online | http://www.dmv.com/ | 410 | 749-7898 | 123 Network |
| 9 | LTGroup | http://www.ltsweb.net/ | 410 | 547-8596 | Network Guys |
| 10 | MD Online | http://www.mdonline.net | 410 | 327-5803 | ABC Networks |
| 11 | MetroNet | http://www.MIN.NET | 410 | 468-0400 | 123 Network |
| 12 | NetGSI | http://www.netgsi.com | 410 | 273-1240 | 123 Network |
| 13 | Quantum Internet | http://www.QIS.NET | 410 | 239-6920 | ITS Inc. |
| 14 | Softaid IS | http://www.SOFTAID.NET | 410 | 290-7763 | Network Guys |
| 15 | Southern MD Inte | http://www.CHESAPEAKE.NET | 410 | 257-5400 | ITS Inc. |
| 16 | TelephoNET Corp | http://www.TELEPHONET.COM | 410 | 427-9000 | ABC Networks |
| 17 | The Columbia Co | http://www.CONNEXT.NET | 410 | 461-5430 | ABC Networks |

**Figure 5.11:** Sample competitive placement spreadsheet created in **Excel**. Note that every company's website is listed. They are inserted as hyperlinks. This allows the network marketer to reference the company's website directly from the spreadsheet. You can use these for people's e-mail addresses as well.

You can make these lists very effective if you include the following:

1. Product Type.

2. What competitive service or product does the company own?

3. Prospect Name.

4. Company's website or person's e-mail address input as a hyperlink:

    - By including the prospect's URL you can engage the prospect's website directly from the competitive list. This reduces research time.

5. Area code:

    - Maintain the area code separately from the phone number for filtering purposes.

6. Phone Number

7. Competitor Name

    - Use standardized names for each competitor for filtering purposes.

84

8. <u>Contact Name</u>

9. <u>Contact information.</u>

10. <u>Miscellaneous</u> information that applies to the industry.

---

○
  **Helpful Hint:** *Hyperlinks in* ***Excel*** *and* ***PowerPoint***

To insert hyperlinks into an **Excel** spreadsheet follow the below steps. Make sure you are linked to the Internet while you perform these steps:

1. Insert

2. Hyperlink...

3. After the window appears, go to your browser.

4. Enter the bookmarks manager and then select the site you want to input, or simply manually type it.

5. Select Copy and then go back to your document. The window will now contain your bookmark as the hyperlink.

6. Select **OKAY**. You have now input a hyperlink and you will be able to go to a site directly from the program.

For e-mail addresses, all you have to do is follow steps 1 & 2 above and then select the drop down menu. "Mailto:" will be an option. Select it and input the e-mail address. (See figure 5.12.)

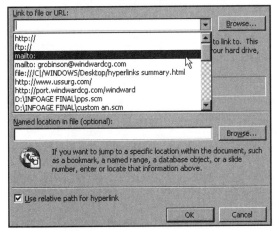

*Figure 5.12:* Excel's insert hyperlink window. Note the "mailto:" above. By selecting this you can send an e-mail directly from an **Excel** spreadsheet by clicking on the e-mail address.

**85**

## **Helpful Hint**: *Creating Autofilters*

To create AutoFilters:
- Highlight all of the cells that you want to filter. Include the row above the highest data-containing row.
- Scroll to the Data pull down menu and select Filter.
- You will be given a choice. Select AutoFilter.

*Figure 5.13:*
**Excel** filtering
menu.

To use AutoFilters:
- Select the drop down above the column you want to view, and highlight a selection.

Note the *drop down icon* at the top of each list in figure 5.14. This is the AutoFilter function and it is helpful in viewing spreadsheets. The AutoFilter categorizes the cells in columns based on content. For example, the product column in figure 5.14 is filtered via the categories in figure 5.13.

| | Company Name | Site | Area Code | Phone | Competitor | Product | Manager Name | E-Mail | Backbone |
|---|---|---|---|---|---|---|---|---|---|
| | Verio | http://www.clark.net | 410 | 995-0550 | ABC Networks | ISP/CONS | Jane Doe | jdoe@company.com | |
| | MD Online | http://www.mdonline.net | 410 | 327-5803 | ABC Networks | ISP/CONS | Jane Doe | jdoe@company.com | |
| | TelephoNET Corp | http://www.TELEPHONET.COM | 410 | 427-9000 | ABC Networks | ISP/CONS | John Doe | jdoe@company.com | |
| | The Columbia Co | http://www.CONNEXT.NET | 410 | 485430 | ABC Networks | ISP/CONS | John Doe | jdoe@company.com | Digex |
| | Toad Computers | http://www.toad.net | 410 | 544-6193 | ABC Networks | ISP/CONS | John Doe | jdoe@company.com | DIGEX/NETAXS/ |
| | Cyber Realm | http://www.cyberrealm.net | 301 | 947-0100 | ABC Networks | 5250 | John Doe | jdoe@company.com | |
| | International Data | http://www.compusnet.com | 301 | 519-0300 | ABC Networks | 5250 | John Doe | jdoe@company.com | CRL |
| | US Net Incorporated | http://www.us.net/ | 301 | 361-6000 | ABC Networks | ISP/CONS | Jane Doe | jdoe@company.com | Sprint/AGIS |

MD ISP / MD CLEC / NOVA CLEC

*Figure 5.14:* A competitive placement list that includes filters. These filters allow for network marketers to view groups by category for prospect review.

## Other *EXCEL-lent Features*

Freeze:  Network marketers can view **Excel** sheets more easily by freezing the column titles in place while scrolling down.  Place

*Figure 5.15:* Freeze menu in **Excel.**

the pointer on the number of the row below the title row and right click. Scroll to Window on the menu bar. (See figure 5.15).

### Protection:

This is a necessary feature for the network marketer. This locks the spreadsheet from changes. This is especially needed when using **Excel** for quotations, justifications, and forecasts, which eventually are forwarded to customers and others. To lock your spreadsheet, select Tools, select Protection,and select the part of the file you would like to protect. This will ask you for a password.

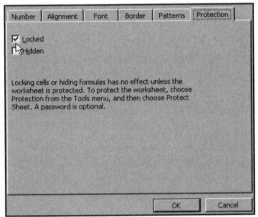

*Figure 5.16:* Protection menu in **Excel**.

Unlocking cells within a locked sheet is sometimes needed because cells need input without allowing access to other cells (justifications, formulas, etc.). To unlock specific cells within a locked sheet, highlight the cell, select Format from the menu bar, select Cells..., click on Protection in the labels that appear and un-check the Locked option. (See figure 5.16).

## Comments in **Word** and **Excel**

Comments are notes that attach to cells in **Excel** and words in **Word** documents. They can be inserted and referenced upon request. They are not always visible, but are shown when placing the pointer on a flagged cell or highlighted word containing a *comment*. *Comments* allow network marketers to include important information in the program without clutter.

## Helpful Hint: *Creating Comments*

To create *Comments:*
- Highlight the cell to which you would like to attach a comment.
- Scroll to the Insert icon.
- Scroll down to Comment.
- Input appropriate information in the block provided.

See figures 5.17 and 5.18 for *comments* illustrations in **Excel** and **Word**.

| | TYPE | Company Name | | | | Area Cod | Phone |
|---|---|---|---|---|---|---|---|
| 3 | | | | | | | |
| 4 | | | | Gerry Robinson: | | | |
| 5 | ISP | DOC NETWORKS | | Performs Network Consulting. | | 301 | 932-7120 |
| 6 | | | | Consumer Internet Access | | | |
| 7 | | | | services as well. | | | |
| 8 | | | | | | | |

**Figure 5.17:** Competitive placement list with comment embedded. Note the flag indicating to the user that more information is contained in the cell. These can help keep the spreadsheet readable. Comments in a competitive placement list can include information such as prospect product descriptions, dates when contacted, contact title and specific phone numbers, additional information like fax numbers, alternate phone numbers, etc.

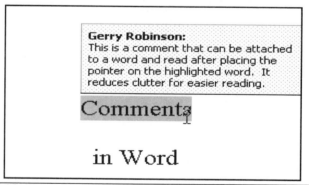

**Gerry Robinson:**
This is a comment that can be attached to a word and read after placing the pointer on the highlighted word. It reduces clutter for easier reading.

Comments

in Word

**Figure 5.18:** This is a comment embedded into a **Word** document. Comments are helpful when editing documents. You can attach comments to words, or groups of words, to suggest different ways to phrase the highlighted selection or to comment on its applicability.

*Comments* are another example of features within the suite of tools on your computer, today, that can help make you more effective. Practice using them and, above all, be creative. You will see your efficiency improve.

## Summary

**Word** and **Excel** are two very valuable programs that help the network marketer with time management. This chapter highlights some of the ways.

**Excel** offers multiple ways to aid the network marketer. ROI's (return on investment) justifications can be automated in spreadsheets. Competitive lists are easy to maintain in **Excel**.

Finally, *comments* is a unique feature that can be used in **Word** or **Excel**.

# Information Age Marketing

"I believe that one of the most powerful forces in the world is the will of the man who believes in himself, who dares to aim high, to go confidently after the things he wants from life ."
  Richard M. DeVos


"There is no security on this earth; there is only opportunity"
  Douglas Mac Arthur


"He who refuses to embrace a unique opportunity loses the prize as surely as if he tried and failed."
  William James


"People's worlds are inversely  proportionate to the size of their fears...that is, the bigger your fears, the smaller your world."
  Mary Charlton Robinson

Many of the hyperlinking methods focused on earlier in this book required the use of the company website in lieu of brochures and mailing materials. This chapter will outline the internal and external website as it should be structured so that the network marketer can maintain a paperless, "postage-less", and "reproduction-less" process.

The definitions of the internal and external website are:

- **Internal website:** This is the site that only the employees of a company can access. It is also commonly known as "Intranet."

- **External website:** This is the site that is available to everyone with access to the world wide web. It is also commonly known as a company's "Homepage" or "Website."

## *Internal Website*

We should first note the many uses of the internal website. Some of them include:

- **Headlines:** News of the day for the company are included here. It serves as a daily newsletter for the company network marketers, updating them on what they need to know.

- **Address Book:** This listing of company employees allows any network marketer to query an employee's contact information via first or last name, extension, office location, or department.

- **Administration:** This site would include links such as:
    - Payroll.
    - Human Resources.
    - Information Technology.
    - Legal department.
    - Travel Department.
    - Upcoming product releases.
    - *Sales and Marketing*.

## *Sales and Marketing*

As the idea for e-marketing tactics grew in my mind, I began to notice the inefficiencies of company's intranets and websites. An example of this is product information, that is, many times, posted on intranets and not available on websites. These sites can't be hyperlinked because customers don't have access to intranets. This information then has to reproduced either by pasting to e-mail, printing, faxing, or mailing and that makes the network marketer inefficient.

Information placement is a company's choice. The decision on where to place the information will become increasingly important as more people are enabled through the Internet. Also, websites increase in size and scope as better technologies become available. Important questions to ask when choosing between whether to place information on an external website or an internal website are:

1. Is the information already presented in sales literature?
2. Is this information valuable if sent to the customer?
3. Is this information sensitive and should it be labeled "internal use only?"
4. Is the information already on the external website in some form and could I create a hyperlink to it?

These questions ensure a proactive approach.

The link tables listed on the next page serve as basic templates on what a network marketer friendly intranet site should contain. Please note that the examples given shouldn't preclude creativity on the company's part; however, if the company includes these basic links, they will be going a long way towards helping their network marketers.

## Intranet SALES & PROSPECTING TOOLS Link Table

### Presentation Tools

1. Downloadable presentations and metrics:
   - Market Specific.
   - Transparency capable.
   - Globally applicable.
   - Attractive graphics.

### Prospecting Tools

1. Global business browser:
   - Query by company name and location.
   - Include detailed financials, contact name and locations.
   - Include competitor names and links to similar information.
   - Leads data base. Query by rep name and territory #.

### Competition

1. Recent product news.
2. Features, advantages, benefits comparisons.
3. Competitor websites.
4. Pricing.
5. Selling tactics.
6. Industry magazine websites.

### *Presentation Tools*

Network marketers are taught to present a message so that it will be understood by the prospect. The best way to accomplish this is to include things of interest. *Market specific* presentations cater messages towards strong markets for a given company. For example, if ABC company sells to the petroleum industry and the utility industry, the website should include individual presentations that address each industry.

For example, the presentation section might look something like this:

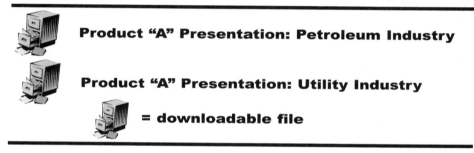

**Product "A" Presentation: Petroleum Industry**

**Product "A" Presentation: Utility Industry**

**= downloadable file**

If there is a possibility, poll top distributors and see what kind of presentations they have in their war cabinet. If there are presentations in the field that could be globally utilized, then include them in this section. Remember that reusing data isn't wrong, it is smart, and network marketers who adopt this philosophy will succeed.

*Transparency capability* is a must in these presentations. If these presentations are being downloaded they need to be able to be reproduced on transparencies to present to the prospect via overhead projector. **PowerPoint** is a great presentation tool with transparency capability.

*Globally applicable* applies to company overviews and press releases. It is important that this material can be used by everybody. Also, don't forget legal issues when making presentations public; such as the use of a customer name without a signed agreement.

*Attractive graphics* ensure that these presentations will serve as templates for new and modified presentations. Remember, the entire company will be showing these presentations to prospects, so it is important that they look professional.

## Prospecting Tools (for people who sell to businesses)

The prospecting page can be one of the most powerful links on your website. It can serve as the online guide for network marketers searching the web for prospects. It can also serve as a quick and easy way to learn about organizations which you are penetrating.

*The Global Business Browser* is a service provided to organizations or individuals. These are information databanks contracted by independent organizations to companies world wide. The information includes:

- Company name.****
- Company location.****
- Financials.
- Contact names.
  - College graduation.
  - Age.
  - Employment History.
  - Likes and Dislikes.
  - Career Track.
  - Associations.
- Satellite offices.
- Competitor names and websites.

(****note the importance of being able to query via this information)

---

### Helpful Hint: *Technology Business Browser*

Along with **Yahoo!** websites such as *Corp Tech* can serve as business and financial information resources for the network marketer.

**CorpTech:** This is the premier site for researching America's technology manufacturers and developers.
http://www.corptech.com/

## *Competition*

Another key section of the sales and prospecting tool link sequence is a competitive section. The secret to assembling a site like this is to include the material sent out to inform distributors about competition. The company doesn't want to recreate the material, but wants to transform the means in which it is communicated.

A competition link in an intranet should, at least, contain the following key components:

- •Recent competitive product news:
  - -What's new with the competition?
  - -What markets are they targeting?
  - -What products are they going to be releasing?
  - -How are they doing financially?
- • Feature, advantage, and benefit comparisons:
  - - Product by product breakdown for network marketer usage (make these downloadable).
  - - Marketing tactics and demonstration techniques versus the competitor's products.
- • Competitor websites.
- • Pricing comparisons.
- • Competitors tactics (many times presented in newsletter form).
- • Websites for industry related news.

## *Training*

Network marketer development is a key to a company's success and is not to be overlooked. By including training on the intranet the training department can guarantee access to important educational material for their distributors. Suggestions on what it should contain are provided below.

### Intranet SALES DEVELOPMENT Links

| **Training material:** | **Training course schedules:** |
| --- | --- |
| • Product sales guide. | • Internal course schedules, including request for attendance forms. |
| • Books to read. | |
| • Training course requirements and timeline. | • Suggested courses available outside the company. |

## Training Material

*Product sales guides* can be downloadable Word, PowerPoint or .PDF files. Companies can use the binder formats used in actual training classes. Companies ensure the information is accurate and up-to-date for their people by including it on their intranet.

*Books to read* suggests books to the team and helps management ensure that ambitious people who read on their free time are informing themselves in ways that match the company's philosophy.

*Training course requirements* serves as the training department's administrative link so that upcoming attendees know what is expected. A *Timeline* is posted to set expectations allowing upcoming students to budget their time so that they can meet expected goals.

## Training Course Schedules

This contains information about both internal and external courses for the network marketer.

## Intranet SALES ADMINISTRATION

- **Pricing and packaging.**
- **Contact information.**
- **Partner information.**
- **Field generated Website Suggestions.**
- **Link to homepage on WWW.**

In this section, standards such as price lists, contact information, partnering company contacts, suggestions, and a link to your external website can be posted.

## External Website

When considering the external website you might think that this would be one of the larger sections of this book. After all, the external website is going to be seen daily by thousands of customers and prospects. It is with that in mind that I want to make the point that this book was not written to serve as a website creation handbook. Its purpose is to provide a template that is useful to the network marketer for companies to keep in mind as they create their sites.

So, you will be happy to read that this next section will be one of the shorter sections in this book. Its length, however, is not an indication of its importance.

First, let's note the key points that make an external website network marketer friendly.

The first point is:

**If the information is worth printing in sales literature, it should be on the external website.**

That is worth repeating. Here it is again:

**If the information is worth printing in sales literature, it should be on the external website.**

The e-marketing process backbone is the hyperlink. If the information is worth mailing to your customer or prospect, then it is certainly worth hyperlinking. It will get there sooner, cheaper, clearer, and more often if it is in hyperlink format. Thus, the first rule of external websites is **If the information is worth printing in sales literature, it should be on the external website.**

The second rule is that it should:

**Be an information map for the customer and the network marketer.**

"Information maps" relate to the flow of the information on the page. An example would be to have all training links on one page so that a customer or prospect can logically educate themselves on that subject. Another example is if you sell product lines a certain way the website should be grouped on your external website that same way.

An example is cars. If you sell cars you might want to have a service link, finance link, and automobile link on each car's page. A prospect who received the link can then research the cars they want to look at and subsequently find out about service and finance.

The third rule of the external website ties to its relationship with the intranet:

**If the information is ever provided to the customer and you are deciding whether to place it on the external or the internal website, ALWAYS PLACE IT ON THE EXTERNAL .**

So many companies make the mistake of including information that is valuable to contacts and network marketers on the intranet. This is inconvenient when needing to send the information to contacts. If it is on the intranet it can't be hyperlinked because the recipient will not be able to access it. As a result, network marketers have to either copy and paste or print the information and send it to the customer. This becomes a waste of time. If it was only on the external website it could be hyperlinked. Remember this when deciding which site to put it on.

The fourth and most important rule is:

## Ensure that every page on your site is named and can be viewed in the browser's address bar.

Websites can be created without naming every page . When this is done the title bar will always show the home page address no matter where you are on the site. An example is:

Company HomePage:  http://www.abc.com

After six clicks deeper into the site, the title bar still reads: http://www.abc.com

The desired result when progressing into a site, is for the address bar to read specific pages. An example is:

Company Home Page:  http://www.abc.com

After one click deeper into the site, the title bar reads: http://www.abc.com/cable.html

After two clicks deeper the title bar reads: http://www.abc.com/cable/listings.html

Notice the difference between the first example and the second. Remember how hyperlinks work. Without a specific name for each page, the network marketer can't utilize the hyperlink because it will always take the contact back to the home page. This removes a valuable tool from their tool box.

## Summary

Two websites exist for the network marketer. They are the Internal and External websites. These are defined as:

- Internal website: This is the site that only the employees of a company can access. It is also commonly known as "Intranet."
- External website: This is the site that is available to everyone with access to the World Wide Web. It is also commonly known as a company's "Home page" or "Website."

The Internal website should contain information to help the network marketer in the marketing process. This includes presentation tools such as **PowerPoint** shows, prospecting tools, and competitive information. Training departments should also have a presence on the internal website for posting training courses, materials, and schedules.

The external website should be created using the following four rules:

- **If the information is worth printing in sales literature, it should be on the external website.**
- **Be an information map for the customer and the network marketer.**
- **If the information is ever provided to the customer, and you are deciding whether to place it on the external or the internal website, ALWAYS PLACE IT ON THE EXTERNAL .**
- **Ensure that every page on your site is named.**

The above four points help in making a network marketer friendly website and ensure that it can be used as outlined in this book.

Website creation has grown exponentially in the past years and many companies have slapped something up just to gain Internet presence. This is harmful with the advent of new browser features such as hyperlinks. It is important to remember how a website can affect network marketers. Consult marketing departments when creating websites. If you have the authority or you can influence your company to make the necessary changes to incorporate what is in this chapter then you should do so. It will change the way you market!

100

# 7

# Hints and Lists

*"The man who does not read good books has no advantage over the man who can't read them."*
*Mark Twain*

*"To win you have to risk loss."*
*Jean-Claude Killy*

*"Working from nine to five provides an average standard of living. It's the work done from five to midnight that really moves you ahead in life."*
*Jay Van Andel*

*"You are the same today as you will be in five years except for two things: The people you meet and the books you read!."*
*Charlie 'Tremendous' Jones*

## Information Age Hints

<u>Corporate Caller ID</u>: Getting to your contacts has become more challenging with the advent of caller ID. Today, company executives can see from where a call is coming. That means that when they see an outside number they are less likely to answer unless they are familiar with it. The way around this is to call the switchboard first and ask to be transferred. Once you are transferred your high level contact sees an internal number on caller ID and is more likely to pick up the call.

<u>Travel Internet</u>: When travelling, you can locate local dial up access points for the Internet by going to your service provider's home site and referencing local service numbers. This can save a lot of money, especially when you are in hotels. If you find yourself travelling to the locations time after time, then create a new dial up shortcut with the new number and place it on your desktop. Call it "Shortcut to Atlanta" or

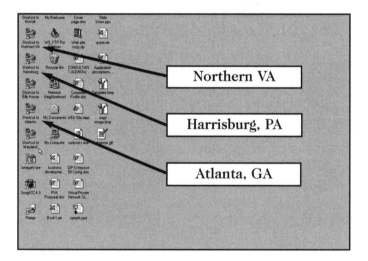

**Figure 7.1:** Desktop showing multiple dialup access icons. These are placed for easy dial up access in frequently traveled cities.

wherever you are travelling. See figure 7.1:

Document Safety: When forwarding **Word** or **Excel** documents or spreadsheets and you wish to prohibit the recipient from the ability to change them, simply print the file as a PDF in Adobe Acrobat's PDFWriter. These file types are read-only files. One other benefit is that they are much smaller in size than their Microsoft cousins and this is advantageous when forwarding via e-mail attachments.

Re-Maximizing Windows on the Desktop: If the Window on your desktop disappears and you don't know where it has gone you shouldn't fear. It is only a keystroke away. Look to the top, sides, or bottom of the screen for the start-up toolbar (see figure 7.2). You will note open programs as icons. Simply, click the icon and the window reappears.

*Figure 7.2:* Start-up toolbar noting two open programs (**Windows Explore**r and **Microsoft Word**). By clicking on these icons you can re-maximize a window that previously was minimized.

## *Web Sites Every Network Marketer Should Know About*

### Directions:

Map Quest This is the most commonly used directions web site. Gives estimated time based on average MPH.
http://www.mapquest.com/

City Guide This is an excellent site with up-to-date directions. Gives estimated time based on average MPH.
http://cg.zip2.com/whowhere/scripts/staticpage.dll?ep=8200&ck=1735754 9&userid=30207140&userpw=xtv0J txAwt8tE FD0C&version=606022&a drVer=901014779&ver=cg0.1

The City Guide site is a long URL address, but all you have to do is type it into your address bar once, travel to the address, and sitemark the site. When you sitemark, save it in the Personal Toolbar and it will always be on

**103**

the screen as a link you can visit.

| | |
|---|---|
| Mapblast | http://www.mapblast.com |
| DeLorme | http://www.delorme.com |
| Yahoo! Maps | http://maps.yahoo.com |
| Mapsonus | http://www.mapsonus.com/ |

## Finding People

| | |
|---|---|
| Bigfoot | http://search.bigfoot.com/SEARCH |

**All Purpose** sites including Find a Business, Finding People's e-mail addresses and contact information, Directions and Maps, Yellow Pages:

| | |
|---|---|
| GTE Superpages | http://superpages.gte.net/ |
| US WEST | http://yp.uswest.com/cgi/search.fcg |
| AT&T Internet Toll Free 800 Directory | http://www.tollfree.att.net |
| Information 555-1212 | http://www.555-1212.com |

## Travel

| | |
|---|---|
| Amtrak | http://www.amtrak.com/ |
| Fodors Travel Online | http://www.fodors.com |
| Leisure Plan | http://www.leisureplan.com |
| Travel Reservations | http://www.reservations.com/ |
| Travelocity | http://www.travelocity.com/ |
| The Weather Channel | http://www.weather.com/twc/homepage.twc |

## Miscellaneous

| | |
|---|---|
| Federal Express | http://www.fedex.com |
| Library of Congress | http://lcweb.loc.gov/homepage/lchp.html |
| Money Online | http://www.money.com |
| USPS | http://www.usps.gov/ |
| DHL | http://www.dhl.com |

## Network Marketing Sites

The most comprehensive site for network marketers, including newsletters, training services, software, and other valuable information.
http://www.mlmdir.com/

This is a large site for the network marketer.
http://www.networkmarketing.com/

Amway Glossary
http://www.mpinet.net/jhoagland/terms.html

Dedicated group of MLMers promoting MLM on the web.
http://www.he.net/

Leap News
Leap is a full service training company offering personal and professional development skills for the novice as well as the experienced networker.
http://www.bobcrisp.com/

Cookie Cutter
Boot Camp on Network Marketing
http://www.kimbell.org

MLM Woman Newsletter
Newsletter for MLM businesswomen.
http://www.www.mlmwoman.com/

Network Marketing tip of the day
These no nonsense tips are designed to help all network marketers start or build a profitable MLM business.
http://home.netcom.com/

Six Figure Income
http://sixfigureincome.com/

Upline Magazine Online
http://www.upline.com/

MLM Yellow Pages
http://www.bestmall.com/mall/

A global organization introducing IMR's and Internet MLM-companies.
http://yi.com/ianm/index.php

## Home Office Help Sites

Home Office
http://www.homeoffice.com

Hot Office.com
http://www.hotoffice.com

## Miscellaneous

Jumbo! The Official Web Site Shareware Site (Over 300,000 free programs)
http://www.jumbo.com/

Shareware.com
http://www.shareware.com

Successful Marketing Strategists
http://www.successful.com

## Customer Contact Research Tool

Hoovers Online
http://www.hoovers.com

- Tools like Hoover's Online offer outstanding information for the network marketer. Included is in-depth financial information; complete lists of officers detailing statistics likes age, career path and income; recent press releases; competitors; and company profiles.

- Subscriptions are often available to online services like Hoover and will provide more detail for a member.